Old DUNDEE

Eric Eunson and Bill Early

First published in the United Kingdom, 2002,
by Stenlake Publishing Ltd
01290 551122
Reprinted 2003, 2006, 2008
www.stenlake.co.uk

ISBN 9781840332162

CONTENTS

In the 1930s the firm of Urquhart & Lindsay merged with Robertson & Orchar. The new company was known by the acronym ULRO. Both firms owned foundries in Dundee and were involved in the design and building of jute works.

INTRODUCTION

Some popular histories of Scotland have claimed that Dundee was founded as a royal burgh in the late twelfth century. However, the very name Dundee is Pictish, a language long dead by that date. It is thought to derive from two words, 'dun' meaning a fortress, and 'deagh', a masculine name translated as 'flame'. In 1792 Dr Small identified the remains of a vitrified fort on the summit of the Law. It is perhaps significant that 'law' is derived from the Norse tongue and also means flame. It is not now possible to know whether the first Dundonians built their fort on the summit of the Law, or on one of the smaller eminences now erased by the city which would have been closer to both the sea and fresh water. It is possible that what Dr Small observed on the Law was a relic of centuries of huge ceremonial pyres which were burned by the Picts on their pagan festivals, such as Beltane or Lughnasad, the festival of the sun god Lugh on 1 August. Later, in Christian times, fires would also have burned on the Law as part of a chain of signal beacons on hilltops around the Scottish coast which were lit in times of national peril.

According to Professor George Stevens, the earliest written evidence of Dundee's history comes not from Scotland, but from Sweden. In the late nineteenth century a runic memorial slab was unearthed at Hogby, East Gotland, which dated from the mid-eleventh century. It recorded the names of fallen warriors and included the line 'At Dundee sank Kari and Buri is also dead'. In 1054 Siward, the Danish Earl of Northumbria, led a force of Anglo–Saxons and Danes into Scotland with the object of deposing Macbeth (1040–57) and replacing him with Malcolm MacDuncan. Siward's army crossed the Forth by way of Stirling, while his fleet sailed into the Tay, and engaged Macbeth's forces on 27 July 1054. Although Siward's army won the victory, it was a pyrrhic one. They sustained heavy casualties, especially among their leaders, and had to withdraw. Some chronicles place this battle at Scone, but writing in the early twelfth century William of Malmesbury also gives the location as Dundee.

Traditionally it is David, Earl of Huntingdon and brother of William the Lion (1165–1213), who is credited with being the founder of Dundee. Although a settlement of some kind was almost certainly already old by this date, it was during the time of Earl David that it came to be a town of some importance. William was intent on expanding the Norman feudal system, introduced to the Lothians by David I (1124–53) and spread throughout Fife by his successor Malcolm IV. Norman influence had a positive effect on all three kings and the feudal system had the effect of creating a strong monarchy. Under it the king would grant a nobleman a parcel of land, on which he was obliged to erect a castle, and to conscript his tenants and servants to the defence of the king on demand. The landscape of east central Scotland was peppered with defensible sites held by an – albeit unpredictably – grateful nobility. William was bent on consolidating his power to the north and granted his brother Dundee as his principal agent in this. The actual grant took place between 1178 and 1182. Dundee was awarded the status of a royal burgh by 1191, and Earl David founded the church of St Mary's in the Field around the same date. A second church, St Clements, stood near the castle and was established before the mid-thirteenth century.

Royal burghs were the first planned towns in Scotland and were laid out by the king's surveyors. The intended inhabitants were Norman merchants, and any village of native Scots would be displaced; thus many Scots were thrown off their land and turned into second class citizens at the will of their own king. Earl David's fortress stood on the Castle Hill, a natural outcrop of rock which once stood where the site of St Paul's Cathedral is today. The choice of this site may imply he was reusing earlier Pictish earthworks in his defences.

In 1296 three Normans, Edward I of England, John Baliol and Robert Bruce began a bitter custody battle over the Scottish crown. According to versions of the semi-legendary tales of his life, Edward's great adversary William Wallace (c.1272–1305) was educated at the High School of Dundee. Some versions also site the start of Wallace's revolutionary career in Dundee, where he is said to have murdered Selbie, son of the Norman governor of the castle in 1297. Wallace was laying siege to the castle later that year when he learned that Edward's army was marching on Stirling. He abandoned the siege of Dundee and proceeded to defeat the English at Falkirk. The following year he was awarded the estate of Dudhope by Alexander Scrymgeour, Constable of Dundee.

During the Wars of Independence (1296–1306) the castle of Dundee changed hands between the two sides several times, and it is believed it was finally destroyed by Robert the Bruce to prevent it falling again into enemy hands. Interestingly, for a town of its subsequent importance a significant fortification was never again erected at Dundee. In 1303 Dundee was attacked by the soldiers of Edward I and many buildings – among them St Mary's Church – were destroyed by fire. The inhabitants of Dundee had lodged their valuables in the church, and many who had taken refuge there were burned alive.

The heart of medieval Dundee was the Seagate and only limited expansion had taken place into the Nethergate before the thirteenth century. In 1325 Robert the Bruce granted Dundee the right to erect its first tollbooth, which stood in Seagate. Two years later he granted a charter to the town confirming its rights as a royal burgh, the original charters having been burned by Longshanks's troops. In 1385 Dundee was again sacked and burned, this time by the forces of Richard II of England.

Lyndsay of Pitscottie tells an extraordinary tale of Dundee which he states took place around 1440. A 'briggant' was brought from Forfar with his 'hail family' (whole family), all of whom were alleged cannibals. The father openly bragged of eating children and young men, claiming 'the younger they war, he esteemed them more tender and delicious'. The whole family were burned, except one female infant who was fostered. However, upon attaining womanhood she is said to have developed the same predilection for human flesh and was also executed. A colourful, if spurious, tale.

Local government of the time was dominated by the merchant guilds, many of whose members were destined to become landed gentry through shrewd marriage. Next in importance came the trade guilds, the members of which banded together to protect both the standards and wages of their crafts. In 1424 James I enjoined the trades of Dundee to choose a wise man as deacon. In 1575 the bakers, cordwainers (shoemakers), glovers, tailors, bonnetmakers, fleshers, hammermen, weavers and dyers joined to become the Nine Incorporated Trades of Dundee, an organisation wielding considerable power until their burgess privileges were revoked in 1846.

Dundee may lay claim to one of the most famous chroniclers of Scottish history, if not the most reliable. Hector Boece was born in the Overgate around 1465, and is thought to have been the son of Alexander Boyis, a city burgess. He was an

3

academic and scholar and in 1533 published his *Historia Gentis Scotorum*. Modern scholars have discredited much of this once oft-quoted work, as Boece rewrote much of medieval Scottish history to glorify the ancestors of James V, not least by creating the entire dramatis personae of Shakespeare's *Macbeth* – witches, Banquo, Macduff and all. By Boece's day Dundee had grown into a thriving metropolis. The frontages of most of the streets in the city centre still bearing the name of 'gate' were almost entirely built up, and encroachments had begun in the backlands of many properties. Incidentally, it is a popular misconception that roads bearing names such as Nethergate are named after entrance gates to the city. In fact these were known as ports; the word road did not come into use in Scotland until the seventeenth century, and gate was the Scots word for a road, derived from the Norse 'gata'. Similarly a land, such as Gardyne's Land off High Street, referred to a tenement and not the ground it stood on.

Noted as a thriving port as early as the thirteenth century, with exports of wool and hides and imports of grain and wine,

the Dundee of 1500 was second in Scotland only to Edinburgh in wealth and importance. However, in 1547 Henry VIII was at the height of his 'Rough Wooing', to coerce Queen Regent Mary de Guise to consent to the marriage of the young Mary Queen of Scots to his son, later Edward VI. Following the disastrous defeat of the Scots at Pinkie that year, the Duke of Somerset sent Sir Andrew Dudley to take Dundee. Broughty Ferry fell, then Dundee, and the English began to fortify the town. Four years of occupation followed before the English were driven out – burning Dundee in their wake – by French forces in the service of Mary de Guise. The Catholic French presence was unwelcome to Dundonians who were eager to adopt the principles of the Reformation, and the Gallic forces maintained an intimidating presence in the city from 1551–60.

In 1598 pestilence began in Dumfries, eventually spreading to Dundee, and plague ravaged the city until 1606, returning again in 1608–09. But the seventeenth century had worse to throw at the beleaguered city. In 1644 Charles I sought to reimpose episcopacy on the Protestant

Scots. Anticipating trouble, the defences of Dundee were strengthened. However, in April 1645 the forces of the Duke of Montrose surprised the defenders of Dundee and took the city, although the duke held it for only a matter of hours before the pursuing Covenanters forced his retreat. The movement of vast numbers of troops frequently led to the spread of plague or typhus, and the country was ravaged by disease again in 1644–45.

The bloody conflict in the name of the Covenant merged with the Civil War. Charles I was executed in 1649 and his family fled into exile. Charles II returned to Scotland and was crowned at Scone on New Year's Day 1651. He lodged in Dundee for some time, before leading a Scottish army to a disastrous defeat at Worcester. In response to the Scots' loyalty to the king, Cromwell sent a punitive expedition north to subdue the country. An army under General Monck besieged Dundee for eight days until the city fell on 1 September 1651. What followed was a gore-drenched fortnight of looting, with a fifth of the city's population slaughtered, an estimated 2,000 men, women and children. Much of the city was again put to the torch and remained in ruins for decades. To refer to the events of 1649–61 as the English Civil Wars is a major misnomer, and one which often prevents Scots from a clear appreciation of some of the most momentous events in their national history.

Dundee struggled to rebuild its trade, hampered by war in Europe which deprived it of many traditional trading partners. Toward 1700 a rich merchant class began to re-emerge. Ships from Dundee plied trade routes to Trondheim, the Low Countries and as far as the Mediterranean. Eighteenth century Dundee was a cosmopolitan place, where the well-to-do could obtain exotic commodities such as silk, citrus fruits and claret. Dundee had long possessed a reputation for the manufacture of coarse cloth, but following the Union of the Parliaments in 1707 Scotland was encouraged to pursue the manufacture of linen. By the 1740s this was well established in Dundee, stimulating a growth of population, fuelled in part by the displacement of rural dwellers from Fife and Tayside caused by improvements in agriculture. Between 1755 and 1801 the population of Dundee rose from 12,400 to 26,800. Wars brought prosperity to the textile trade, and the Napoleonic Wars created a huge demand for sailcloth, sacking and – presumably – shrouds.

Following the French Revolution radical views began to circulate in Britain, and Dundee was something of a hotbed of dissent. In 1790 the Whig Club of Dundee spoke in praise of the Revolution, calling it 'the triumph of liberty and reason, over despotism, ignorance and superstition'. But then they weren't living in brutal post-revolutionary France.

Old DUNDEE

circa 1450

HUGH M. ASHCROFT. '84

The year 1792 saw riots in several Scottish towns and cities, and a Tree of Liberty was erected at the Town Cross of Dundee by a mob proclaiming 'Liberty and Equality'. In 1793 Dundee Unitarian minister T. F. Palmer played a major role in a Friends of the People convention in Edinburgh and was transported to Botany Bay for fourteen years. Another suffragist ringleader was Dundonian George Mealmaker, transported for seventeen years in 1797. Dundee can boast that it has always produced citizens willing to speak zealously for reform.

Steam power first began to be used in the linen industry in the 1790s and in 1836 David Baxter built Dundee's first powerloom factory. Handloom weaving could be heavy work, and was a male-dominated cottage industry; the introduction of factory weaving produced a huge shift towards a female dominated workforce.

Jute, an Asian plant of the genus *Corchorus* whose bark yields a rough fibre used for making twine and rope and weaving into sacking, was first imported to Britain by the British East India Company in 1791. In Dundee the manufacture of jute textiles had small beginnings, but by the 1830s production was rocketing. Further impetus for the growth of the industry was provided by the Crimean War (1853–56) and many jute and linen factories added massive new works in this period.

Child labour was used extensively in the jute and linen mills, and in 1834 only one in thirteen Dundee children received any formal education. Despite the passing of a series of Factory Acts, it was not until 1833 that government inspectors were employed to ensure any regulations regarding the treatment of factory workers were actually enforced. The employment of women and children kept wages low, and children were routinely beaten in the mills until the 1890s. An Act of 1844 introduced the half-time system of education for children between the ages of eight and fourteen employed in the mills, whereby they worked a six hour shift and then attended school for a similar period. In 1900 there were some 5,000 girls between the ages of 12 and 14 working either as half timers or wholly excused attendance in school, providing they agreed to some education outwith working hours. Some vestiges of the half-time system still lingered until its eventual abolition in 1936.

Its dependence on textile manufacture led to Dundee being referred to as a 'women's town' and in the 1901 census there were three women for every two men in the city. Male unemployment was high, and a son or husband unable to find work would remain at home and perform the housework. Twenty years later it was revealed that 24% of married women in Dundee worked, four times the same statistic in Glasgow. Indeed, the middle class Dundee Social Union did not campaign for higher pay or improved housing or sanitation, but for more job opportunities for men.

For males the largest source of employment in the city was the shipyards. With its long-established tradition of maritime trade, shipbuilding had probably been carried out from an early date, but did not become a major industry until the late eighteenth century. In 1814 the first Dundee-built steamship, the *Tay*, was launched at the yard of James Smart. By this time there were six shipbuilders with yards stretching from Yeaman Shore and along the site of Dock Street. Although Dundee became the largest shipbuilding centre on the east coast, the industry was subject to economic vagaries and in the 1920s was in a very depressed state. The collapse of the local whaling industry in 1914 saw the demise of all but two yards, and after 1920 only the Caledon remained in business. The jute trade also experienced a severe slump after the First World War and by 1921 the mills and factories were almost silent. Dundee had been losing overseas customers for jute since the 1850s, ironically largely due to Dundonian interests which had begun the manufacture in India itself. By 1900 the trade was kept deceptively buoyant by the domestic market and customers in the United States and Latin America. A combination of trade depression and the loss of domestic customers to Indian competition meant hungry years for the jute industry through the 1930s, although some 28,000 were still employed.

The 1919 Housing Act paved the way for the development of council housing, and Dundee was the first city in Scotland to embark on a major building programme. The 'garden suburb' of Logie was constructed between 1919 and 1921, with Craigiebank begun in 1920 and Taybank the following year. By 1924 houses in both The Glens and Stirling Park were also occupied. The Act had been intended to pave the way for slum clearances, but in Dundee, gripped by economic gloom and largely dependant on low paid female breadwinners, the rents of the new houses were too high to be affordable to those most in need. In 1921 work began on a major new city artery, the Kingsway. It was the brainchild of Dundee's city architect Frank Thomson, and reflected his foresight in anticipating dramatically increasing traffic volumes – something that other cities failed to recognise for decades to come.

In 1939 some 28,000 were still employed in jute, but following the war employment opportunities began to diversify. The first industrial estate beyond the Kingsway opened in 1946, with Timex being the first major employer to take up residence. By 1964 it had been joined by National Cash Registers and Morphy Richards. At this point only 18,000 were employed in jute, and the industry's low wages (compared to the new factories) meant that jute manufacture was increasingly dependant on immigrant labour from India and Pakistan. The trade continued to contract in size each year, and it was only a switch to man-made fibres, notably polypropylene, which kept the remaining factories afloat.

The 1960s saw the textile and jute industries diminish into insignificance, but their loss made little impact due to booming manufacturing and service sectors. However, the late 1970s and early 1980s saw one major employer after another quit the city. Perhaps most memorable was the closure of the Timex plant in 1993, the announcement of which led to eight months of increasingly confrontational strike action.

The arrival of the *Discovery* in Dundee in 1986 heralded a new identity for the city, that of tourist destination. The Verdant Works jute museum followed and joined existing assets like the McManus Galleries, an institution worthy of any great city, in drawing visitors from all over the globe. On the peripheries of the city failed 1960s housing estates are currently being revamped and irredeemable slums in the sky have been sent crashing to the ground, beginning with Ardler in 1993. The Millennium saw the destruction of the universally loathed Overgate Centre and a graceful new mall rise in its stead. With the completion of the swish new Debenhams department store, the age of the personal shopper has arrived in Dundee.

Before 1713 unregulated ferries provided an irregular service between various points near Dundee and the Fife shore. In that year the Guildry of Dundee established a more reliable service between Dundee and Sea Myles, which later acquired the name of Newport. The sailing boats and pinnaces employed remained privately owned until the service passed into the control of the Tay Ferry Trustees in 1819. The first steamship to be employed on the crossing was the *Union*, which was used from 1820 to 1836. In 1870 the service came under the jurisdiction of the Dundee Harbour Trustees. This *c*.1902 view shows the *Dundee*, which entered service in 1875. She was sold to the Tay Steamboat Company for pleasure sailings in 1917, and was later employed on the Queensferry passage on the Forth. She was scrapped after a long career in 1952.

Motor vehicles on the deck of the Dundee ferry *Sir William High*, with a perilously overloaded carrier's lorry in the foreground. Built in 1924 at Dundee's Caledon yard, the *Sir William High* plied the Tay until 1952 when she was sold to a Nigerian buyer. This picture was taken in 1929, the year in which Newport Pier was doubled in width and extended to cope with the increased level of vehicular traffic. At the same time the ferry service increased in frequency from hourly to half-hourly.

The *Sir William High* was joined on the Dundee passage by the *B. L. Nairn* in 1929. She too was a Caledon-built vessel and the last paddle steamer to be employed as the Dundee ferry. She was fitted with radar in 1948, a similar improvement being made to the *Sir William High* in 1949. By 1957 she was in need of extensive repairs, with a fractured drive shaft and much of her plating in need of replacement. She was refurbished, but retained only as a stand-by vessel. The *B. L. Nairn* was scrapped in 1966 following the completion of the Tay Road Bridge, which ended forever the days of the 'Fifies'.

Even in the early 1930s the volume of traffic was threatening to turn the ferry piers at Dundee and Newport into bottlenecks, and Dundee Town Council proposed a road bridge across the Tay as early as 1921. However, an additional ferry boat was a much cheaper option and the MV *Abercraig*, seen here at Newport in the mid-1960s, was introduced in 1939. She was built by Fleming & Ferguson of Paisley and was the first of the Dundee ferries to be fitted with radar in 1947.

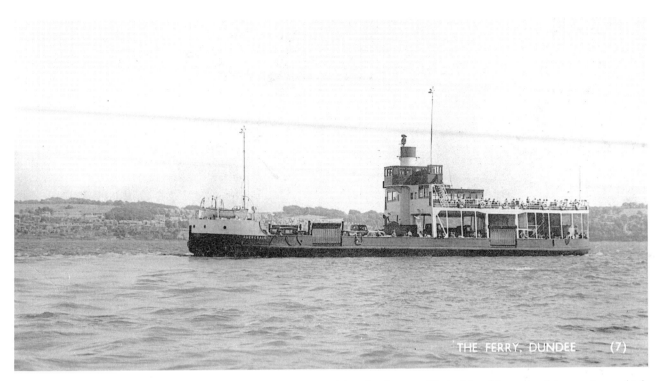

THE FERRY, DUNDEE (7)

The *Abercraig* on open water around 1952. She was powered by the German Voth Schneider propulsion system which made her more manoeuvrable than the older paddle steamers, an asset in the treacherous currents of the Tay. However, she experienced frequent propeller problems, and was laid up on numerous occasions during the war when spares from Germany were unobtainable.

After World War II the Fifies were once again toiling to cope with both the volume of traffic and the increasing size of commercial vehicles, especially when the *Sir William High* and *B. L. Nairn* were on the crossing. Another vessel was required and in 1951 the Caledon Shipbuilding & Engineering Company launched the *Scotscraig*, a twin screw vessel with a diesel electric engine. From 1963 onwards passengers aboard the ferries watched as the concrete pillars of the new road bridge rose from the Tay. After the bridge opened in 1966 the ferries were retired to Victoria Dock. Both the *Abercraig* and *Scotscraig* were ultimately sold to a Maltese buyer. By the early 1970s the *Scotscraig* was at the bottom of the Mediterranean, the *Abercraig* eventually lying derelict in Marsa Harbour. Despite attempts to have her returned to Dundee, the last of the Fifies was broken up in 1995.

In October 1864 a public meeting of parties eager to see the construction of a rail bridge across the Tay was held in Dundee. Provost Parker presented the engineer Thomas Bouch who announced the project would be 'a most ordinary undertaking' and estimated the cost to be £180,000. Parliamentary approval was granted in 1870 and in 1871 the contract was awarded to Charles Bergue & Co. of London. The foundation stone was laid at Wormit on 22 July 1871. Construction was fraught with problems, however, as Bouch had identified solid rock where there was nothing but sand, and the bridge had to be redesigned. In 1873 Bergue died and the work was completed by Hopkins Gilkes & Co. of Middlesborough. Numerous lives were lost during construction, and the bridge took twice the proposed three years to complete. A storm in February 1877 marooned 54 workmen for a terrifying night and caused extensive damage; it was a foretaste of events to come.

The first engine passed over the bridge on 26 September 1877. This was followed by an official inaugural train on 31 May 1878, hauled by the locomotive *Lochee* and comprising 23 first class carriages containing 1,500 passengers. Among them were John Stirling, chairman of the NBR and the recently knighted Thomas Bouch, both of whom received the freedom of Dundee. On 28 December 1879 the 5.27 p.m. from Burntisland was crossing the bridge in fierce weather when the central portion collapsed into the Tay, taking the locomotive and carriages with it. Not one of the 75 passengers or four crew escaped. This photograph was taken shortly after the disaster and shows the fallen girders beached near Wormit.

The salvaged tender, photographed at Dundee by Valentine's. Bouch, or Bodge as he may be better remembered, had a history of cost-cutting which had proved problematic in the past, and was immediately stripped of his commission to design a new bridge across the Forth. Personal effects belonging to victims of the disaster continued to be recovered from the Fife shore for months afterwards, and the McManus Galleries contain a poignant selection of items, among them a letter and a lady's glove. A section of the wrecked bridge found a new use when it was again placed across the Tay at Caputh village in Perthshire.

The present Tay Rail Bridge was designed by W. H. Barlow and built between 1882 and 1887. The ironwork was made by Sir William Arrol's foundry in Glasgow. Two miles and 364 yards in length, it was in its day the longest bridge in the world. Beams from the old bridge were recycled as outside girders in some of the 72 approach spans. This picture dates from around 1930.

The Tay Bridge opened to goods traffic on 13 June 1887 and passenger services commenced a week later. The photographer who captured this 1950s view of Dundee may have been standing on the open platform of a goods train brake van.

Tay Bridge station was opened with the first Tay Bridge in 1878, and looked much the same as it does in this Edwardian view until it was radically modernised in the early 1980s.

By the 1730s the British government had grown wary of the nation's dependence on imported supplies of whale oil, and offered generous bounties to encourage the establishment of an indigenous whaling fleet. The Dundee Whale Fishing Company was set up around 1750 and by the end of the century the city had a fleet of four whaling vessels. By 1811 its fleet numbered six, second in Scotland only to Peterhead. From 1820 to 1850 the industry was in decline, but in the 1850s the rapidly-expanding jute industry created an increase in demand for whale oil, which was used to soften the raw jute fibres, a process known as batching. In the same period the Alexander Stephen Shipbuilding Co. began to develop a well-deserved reputation for building large wooden whaling vessels (it was found that wooden ships better withstood the pressure of the Arctic ice than those with metal hulls). Stephen's yard was established in the mid-1840s, and when he left for Glasgow in 1869 it was taken over by the Dundee Shipbuilders Co. By the 1870s Dundee was the supreme whaling port in Britain, but in the following decade mineral oil began to replace whale oil in jute batching. Whalebone now became the profitable commodity, but by this time over-exploitation had seriously affected the Arctic whale population. A single expedition of four whalers left Dundee for the Antarctic in 1892, but the enterprise was a failure and was never repeated. By 1913 only two whalers remained at Dundee and the industry was abandoned in 1914.

The Dundee Shipbuilders Co.'s expertise in building whalers made them an obvious choice for Captain Robert Falcon Scott when he sought a yard to construct a custom-made vessel for a voyage of exploration to the Antarctic. The keel of the *Discovery* was laid in March 1900 and she was launched at Dundee on 21 March 1901. Her frames were made from English oak, lined with Riga fir; the sides of the ship were 26 inches thick and her bow was reinforced with steel plates. She sailed from London on 31 July 1901 for a three year scientific expedition, and withstood well immense pressure among the ice floes. She was subsequently bought by the Hudson Bay Co. as a merchant vessel, and later spent over 40 years as a Sea Scout training ship on the Thames. The *Discovery* was given to the Maritime Trust in 1979 and returned to Dundee in 1986.

The *Terra Nova* was built in 1884 by the Dundee Shipbuilders Co. and was the last whaler to be constructed at Dundee. In 1904 the Admiralty sent her as part of a relief mission to rescue Scott (inset) and his crew from the ice-bound *Discovery*. When Scott had planned his ill-fated expedition to the South Pole in 1909 he had hoped to once again employ the *Discovery*, but the Hudson Bay Co. refused to sell her. With a 25 year history of Arctic whaling the *Terra Nova* was his second choice and he bought her for £12,500. The expedition ended in tragedy with the last of the party perishing in March 1912 when tantalisingly close to achieving their goal. The *Terra Nova* was lost off Greenland in World War II. She sprung a bad leak and it was decided to sink her, but it took 23 rounds of three inch gunfire from the US Coastguard cutter *Atak* to finish the job.

This 1906 image was taken on board the Dundee whaler *Morning* and is reproduced from a postcard entitled 'Esquimaux at Saunder's Island, Greenland'. In the winter of 1903 the *Morning* was sent to the Antarctic to relieve Scott's *Discovery* expedition. As well as bringing mail and supplies, she took off those of the party who where no longer well enough to remain there. Among them was Ernest Shackleton, who is said to have wept as she sailed away. In 1904 the *Morning* joined the *Terra Nova* on the second expedition to relieve Scott.

This picture of Etah natives of Greenland was also taken on board the *Morning*. The relish with which they seem to be enjoying their meal of raw seal fins suggests that either hunger is a great appetiser or revulsion is a conditioned response! The picture was one of some 600 taken by photographer Sandon Perkins, who sailed as a passenger on the *Morning* during a whaling voyage to the Arctic in 1906.

Edinburgh Slip,
Dundee

The steam yacht *Velocity* is recorded as plying between Edinburgh and Dundee in 1821, a route that was soon extended to link the two cities with Aberdeen. The railways had long since removed the need for – and viability of – such a service by the time this view of the old Edinburgh slip was taken in 1905. At the time it was being used as the starting point for pleasure sailings on the Tay. The *Bonnie Dundee* was built at Montrose in 1890 and was captained by James Tares. She made cruises to Bridge of Earn and Balmerino for the price of sixpence, and passengers spent an hour and a half ashore. The last cruise from Dundee to Perth was made by the *Tay Lady* in 1948.

This 1905 view is now almost unrecognisable, the docks and buildings having vanished under the landfall area of the Tay Bridge. The King William IV Dock lay beyond the warehouses in front of the Royal Arch. In the early nineteenth century the existing tidal harbour was prone to silting and was ill-suited to Dundee's expanding trade. Provost Riddoch commissioned the celebrated engineer Robert Stephenson to draw up plans for a replacement, but other town council members accused him of self-interest and commissioned a second set of plans from Thomas Telford. The ensuing political wrangle ran for several years, the Telford scheme finally being adopted. This involved turning the upper tidal harbour into a wet dock controlled by sluices, and the King William IV Dock was completed in 1825. The Earl Grey Dock, in the foreground, was also designed by Telford and adapted from the eastern tidal harbour. The work was supervised by Dundee harbour engineer James Leslie and completed in 1834.

These torpedo boats photographed in the Earl Grey Dock in 1905 were the vanguard of a naval presence at Dundee which was to last for the next half century.

The Sunlit Docks, Dundee.   689

Dundee's modest fishing fleet, berthed in King William IV Dock around 1910. Despite their maritime tradition Dundonians never seem to have shown much interest in being fishermen, relying instead on supplies of fish from the ports of the Angus coast. Fishwives from as far away as Auchmithie walked the 48 mile round trip, laden with fish to sell in the Greenmarket. Dundee supported a thriving curing industry in the mid-nineteenth century, although it had no fishing boats at all in this period. By the late 1920s it had a fleet of nine steam trawlers and eleven sail boats, based in the Camperdown Dock. There was also an annual sprat fishery in the Tay from December to February. Most of the sprats were sent for canning, but after more than a third of the 1929 catch had to be sold as manure following a sharp fall in demand the fishery was abandoned.

An atmospheric shot of what was almost certainly a jute ship, taken in Victoria Dock in 1910. Construction of the Victoria Dock by James Leslie began in 1833, again to plans by Thomas Telford. However, although the adjoining Camperdown Dock was completed in 1865, work on the Victoria Dock was mothballed for some 30 years. It resumed in 1869 and the dock was completed to Telford's plans in 1875.

The Docks, Dundee,

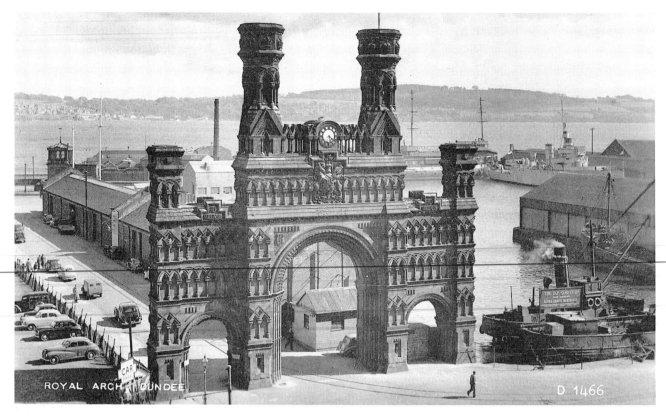

When Queen Victoria visited Dundee in 1844, the harbour engineer James Leslie was commissioned to design a triumphal arch for the occasion. There was no time to erect one in stone and the first Royal Arch was built of wood. A more permanent arch made of sandstone was erected in 1850 to a design by the architect and sculptor J. T. Rochead, who also designed the Wallace Monument near Stirling. The Royal Arch was torn down in 1964 in preparation for the construction of the Tay Road Bridge. The little dredger on the right of this 1955 picture belonged to the Tay Sand & Gravel Company.

Built in 1824, the frigate *Unicorn* is the oldest surviving British warship afloat. She was berthed in King William IV Dock in 1873, and in 1906 became the training ship for the local Royal Naval Volunteer Reserve, a group of whom are shown in this contemporary photograph. The wooden roof over her deck was added at the time of her conversion in 1906. During the last war HMS *Unicorn* served as the headquarters of the Naval Officer in Charge, Dundee. She was moved to Camperdown Dock in 1962. In recent years she has been rescued from decrepitude and is currently under restoration.

A flotilla of C-Class submarines arrived in the Tay on 11 July 1908, and the Admiralty entered into negotiations to use part of Dundee docks as a submarine base. Initially this was to be from October 1908 to August 1909, but the base at Dundee was maintained until the outbreak of war in 1914. Apparently the naval officers at the base were not popular with local traders as they were tardy in settling their bills!

One of the techniques of war practised by the submarines on the Tay was known as the towing programme. This involved a submarine being towed by a trawler which would act as a lookout ship, releasing the sub when an enemy U-boat was sighted. On 23 June 1915 the C24, commanded by Lieutenant Taylor, one of the submarines formerly based at Dundee, sank the U40, the first German submarine casualty of the war.

HMS *Vulcan*, seen here off Dundee in 1908, was brought from Nore (an area of the Thames near Sheerness) and served as a dormitory and tender for the submarine crews. At the outbreak of war in 1914 the *Vulcan* and the 7th Flotilla of submarines were transferred to war stations at Leith.

The 7th Flotilla returning to Dundee from exercises, with one of the Tay dredgers in the background. When war broke out in 1939 a depot ship and six submarines were on a courtesy visit to the Tay and began their war duty from Dundee. One of these, the *Oxlex*, was the first British submarine to be lost in the North Sea, a victim of friendly fire. By 1945 Dundee had become a significant submarine base and hosted subs from Poland, France, the Netherlands and Norway, as well as Britain.

The Dundee, Perth & London Shipping Company's steamer *Perth* in Camperdown Dock in 1910. The DP&LS Co. was founded in 1798 and steadily developed an impressive fleet of sailing and later steamships, handling both cargo and passengers. The *Perth* was the fourth of the company's vessels to bear the name, and was built in 1890 by W. B. Thomas of Dundee. Renamed *Arbroath* in 1917, she was requisitioned for transport duties in the Mediterranean in 1918. After a brief period running between Southampton and Le Havre on Admiralty duties, she was returned to her owners in 1920. They sold her the same year and she ended her days in Turkey, where she was broken up in 1959.

HMS *Cairo* and four destroyers, *Valentine*, *Walpole*, *Wolfhound* and *Windsor*, arrived in Dundee on 2 October 1933 and remained for seven days. The *Cairo* was berthed at the east end of King George Wharf, and the destroyers in Camperdown and Victoria Docks. Upon their arrival the ships' officers were treated to a civic reception and luncheon hosted by the Corporation and Harbour Trustees.

A view of the Stannergate Shipyard, part of the Caledon Company's complex, dating from 1920, the same year the Dundee Shipbuilding (formerly Shipbuilders) Company was wound up, making Caledon the last shipyard in Dundee. W. B. Thomson had acquired the Tay Foundry at Stobswell in 1867 and in 1874 bought a stretch of shore frontage and set up a shipyard. His first commission was a steam yacht for the Earl of Caledon, in honour of whom he named the yard. In 1896 he took over the shipyard of the Lilybank Foundry, and the Stannergate yard seen here was laid out during the Great War. The new yard was capable of building ships up to 560 feet keel.

Seen here leaving the Caledon yard in 1953, the Ardrossan-registered *Baron Kilmarnock* was the largest vessel to have been built on the east coast of Scotland at that time. During both world wars the Caledon yard worked exclusively on Admiralty commissions, both building and repairing ships. In the inter-war period the yard built several passenger liners for the Blue Funnel and Ellerman Lines, and in 1954 launched an even bigger vessel than *Baron Kilmarnock*, the 12,000 ton Norwegian-registered *Storeas*. Along with the rest of Britain's shipyards, the Caledon experienced competition from cheaper overseas yards and eventually succumbed to closure in 1982.

Heart of the City

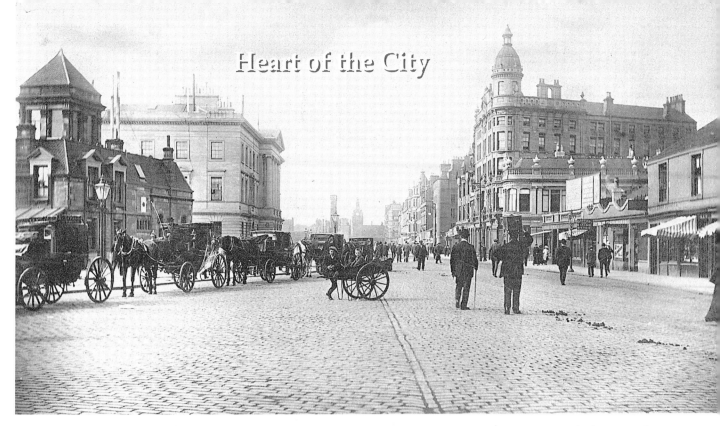

The skyline of this 1909 view of Dock Street is now dominated by the Tay Road Bridge and its access roads, but the foreground at least is still recognisable. The ambience, however, has changed beyond recognition and the cobbled street, rank of hansom cabs and promenading gentlemen have been replaced by four lanes of speeding traffic on one of the city's main arterial roads. The building sporting a turret on the right was the Sailors' Home, designed in 1881 by David Maclaren. It was built charitably to keep visiting sailors from the temptations of the fleshpots and shebeens of Dundee.

On 1 April 1840 the railway from Arbroath to Dundee was opened with a terminus in Trades Lane. This was moved to Dock Street in 1857 and the new station was called Dock Street until 1858 when it was renamed Dundee East. This view of the building dates from 1905 and bears the epithet 'The Black Hole', bestowed upon it by many Dundonians. Dundee East closed on 5 January 1959 and was subsequently demolished.

CUSTOM HOUSE, DUNDEE.

Dundee's neoclassical Custom House was erected in 1843 at a cost of £8,000 and was occupied by administrative offices for the collection of shore dues and customs and excise duties. It also housed the chambers of the Harbour Board. The building was designed by James Leslie and John Taylor. James Leslie (1801–89) was born at Coates near Largo, Fife and was the son of John Leslie (1766–1832), one of the most celebrated scientists of his age. By 1825 Leslie was harbour engineer at Dundee and it was he who supervised the construction of the Earl Grey, King William IV and Victoria Docks. He also designed several railway viaducts in Tayside and Fife.

Some of the buildings in this 1909 view of Dock Street remain, but the skyline has been drastically altered by the Tay Road Bridge. The King William IV Dock can be glimpsed on the left, while in the foreground are tracks which were part of a dockside railway which employed small pug engines to transport cargoes to and from ships.

92. Corner of Old Greenmarket, The Site of Caird Hall, Dundee.

The Greenmarket developed on the site of part of the medieval churchyard of St Clements. This was rendered obsolete when Mary Queen of Scots gifted the city the land which became the Howff Cemetery in 1564. In the nineteenth and early twentieth century the Greenmarket was Dundee's fish market, and from 1882 was let to the showmen attending the Lady Mary's Fair. The Corporation began acquiring property here in 1914 in anticipation of the clearance of the area to erect the Caird Hall. Considering its proximity to the docks, one might assume the Crown Hotel, with its gable to the street, was a rough establishment, but apparently its last proprietrix, Mrs Steel, had a no-nonsense attitude and kept an orderly house! The business was founded in 1840 as Campbell's Crown Hotel and Coach Office.

The Caird Hall was completed in 1922 and obliterated the old Greenmarket. However, until 1934 a market in second-hand goods was allowed to continue three times a week on Tuesday, Friday and Saturday in the bowels of the ostentatious new civic centre. The Lady Mary Fair was also abolished in 1934.

Old Greenmarket, Dundee
On this Site has been built the magnificent Caird Hall

Seen here in the early years of last century, the Royal Arch tearoom stood at 19 Dock Street. Dock Street once had a handsome river frontage including shipping offices and popular pubs, among them the Castle and Harbour bars. Several fine buildings remain and it is much to be hoped that developers with fill unsightly gap sites with sensitivity.

Opposite: This impressive Sentinel steam lorry was built in the 1920s for Robert Taylor, coal merchant and ship owner. The business was founded in 1880 at premises in Commercial Street and moved to the Yeaman Shore two years later.

The Alexandra Fountain at the foot of South Union Street was presented to the city by Provost Longair to commemorate several brief visits by Queen Alexandra during the first decade of the twentieth century. She alighted at Dundee while travelling by sea to Denmark to visit her family. The fountain survived the wholesale destruction of its surroundings in the early 1960s, but for many years stood in the middle of a forlorn wasteland. It has recently been restored and is now a feature of Discovery Quay.

South Union Street, Dundee

The tower of the Caledonian Railway's Dundee West station can be seen on the left of this 1907 view. The station was designed in 1889 by Thomas Barr, the Caledonian's chief engineer, in a style with an identity crisis between Gothic and baronial. It replaced an earlier station built by the Scottish Central Railway in 1867, and finally closed on 3 May 1965. On the opposite side of the street is the imposing frontage of Mather's Hotel, erected in 1900. Mather's was established in 1869 at 69 Murraygate before moving to Whitehall Street in 1887. In 1981 it became the Tay Centre Hotel, but what was once a prestigious establishment became a DHSS hostel in 1996. It was gutted by fire the following year and is presently boarded up and facing an uncertain future.

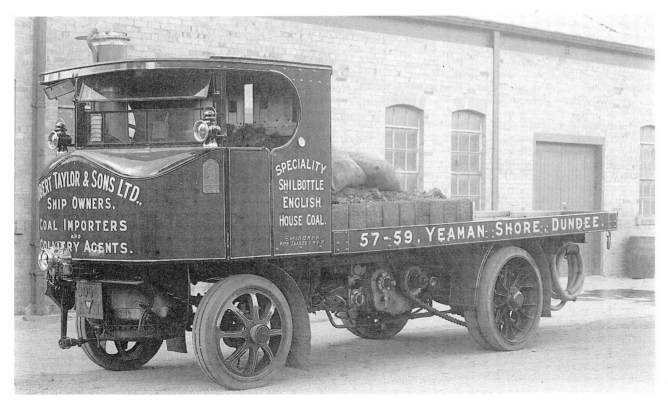

Contemporary art nouveau lettering on the outside, and cutting-edge Edwardian hairdressing technology on the inside of L. Hill Rennie's shop at 7 Union Street. It advertised high class ladies' and gents' hairdressing, manicure, chiropody and face massage saloons, while its 'hairwork' department insisted all wigs were made on the premises by experienced workmen and only used the finest hair and materials. The hairdryer, shown in the right-hand picture, was described as 'the only way of drying ladies' hair which is highly recommended by the health authorities and absolutely prevents catching cold after shampooing'.

Opposite bottom: David Drysdale founded a saddlery business at 6 Castle Street in 1891. In 1932 the shop moved to these premises at 3 Exchange Street, where this popular Dundee business remained until closure in 1979.

Frain's china shop in Castle Street occupied the former Theatre Royal which was opened in 1810. It was Dundee's first custom-built theatre and was the work of city architect Samuel Bell. Apart from the Trades' Kirk it is the best surviving example of his work, although only the facade with its bust of Shakespeare remains. It is currently undergoing restoration and is to be retained as the frontage of a new building. Castle Street was created in 1785 by blasting through the Castle Rock, the site of Dundee's medieval fortress.

The Theatre Royal was superseded by Her Majesty's Theatre and Opera House in Seagate which opened in 1885. St Paul's Cathedral can be seen in the background of this 1903 picture. It was designed by the architect Sir George Gilbert Scott, famous for his use of the Gothic, and was completed in 1898 some twenty years after his death. The cathedral stands on the actual site of the Castle Rock.

The facade of Her Majesty's Theatre *c.*1910, when its management advertised it as 'the premier theatre of the town and district' and claimed that it showed 'first class London productions only'. Her Majesty's later became a cinema and was destroyed by fire in 1941. The site was then occupied by a new cinema which eventually became the Cannon, itself demolished in the 1990s.

Flatbed carts like this Edwardian example were once a ubiquitous sight on the streets of Dundee, and were the principal means of transporting raw materials and finished goods to and from the mills. This one belonged to Andrew Henry, who founded his contractor's business in 1882 in Stobswell Road. The following year he transferred to 61 Trades Lane, at which point he went into partnership with a Mr Robbie. By 1903 directories list only Andrew Henry, and by 1908 he had moved next door to 59 Trades Lane. The business ceased trading in 1936.

DUNDEE'S GREAT FIRE, 19th and 20th July 1906. Damage, over £400,000.
Remains of six-storey Bonded Warehouse, shewing Boyd-Wilson Patent Cement-cased Pillars and three concrete floors undamaged by fire and still intact, except where smashed by falling walls. With the exception of crumbling walls, this is the only part of all the buildings left standing.
The Portland Cement used was manufactured by *I. C. Johnson & Co., Ltd.*, London and Gateshead.

The conflagration known as 'Dundee's great fire' began at around 6.20 p.m. on Thursday 19 July 1906. The blaze is thought to have started in the roof or top floor of Watson's No. 4 whisky bonded warehouse, at the corner of Seagate and the aptly named Candle Lane. The bond was full at the time and the blaze quickly got out of control as burning spirit passed freely through walls and under doors, spreading to a neighbouring whisky bond belonging to John Robertson. Both buildings were utterly destroyed, along with adjoining premises including a provisions warehouse belonging to the Scottish Wholesale Co-operative Society and Stewart Robertson's warehouse of fireclay goods. Two nearby jute warehouses were destroyed when their roofs were ignited by falling embers. The total cost of the damage was estimated at £400,000.

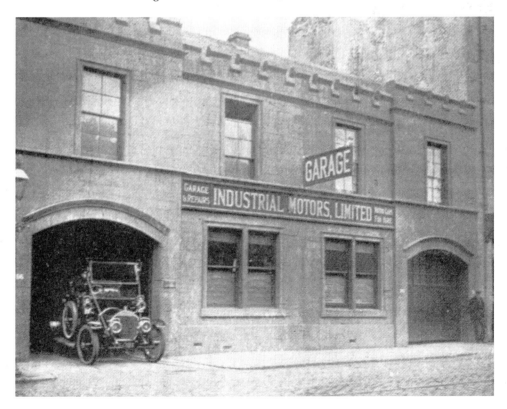

Industrial Motors' castellated garage in Seagate *c.*1910. In addition to their motor engineering department, the garage also carried out an extensive motor hire business, advertising private cars, touring cars and a fleet of motor charabancs.

31

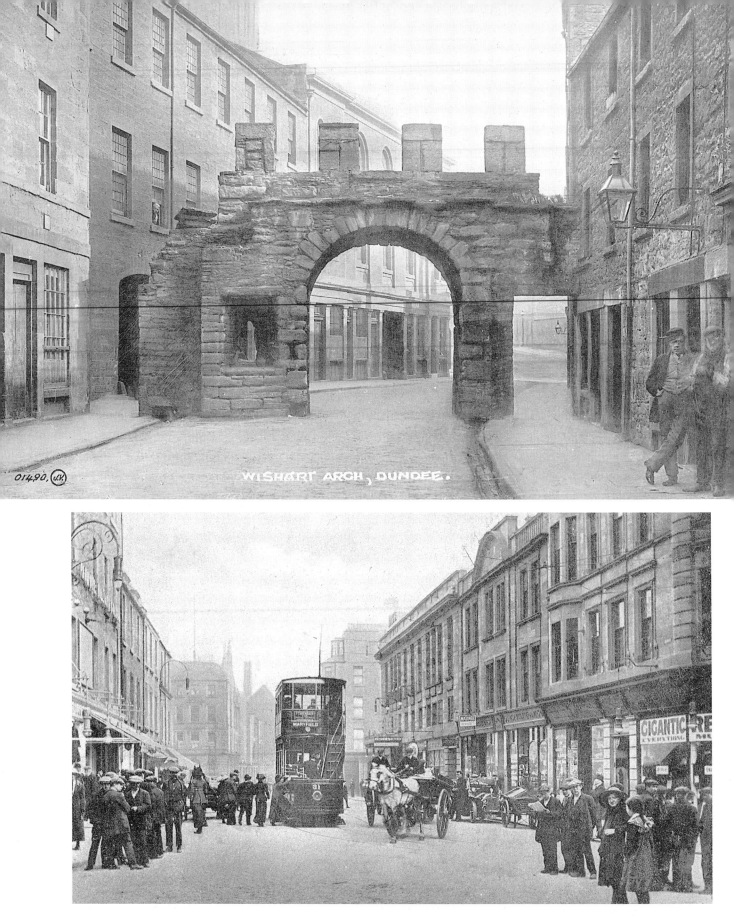

WISHART ARCH, DUNDEE.

The building on the extreme left of this 1910 view of the Cowgate is believed to have been constructed in 1790. Tradition maintains that Robert Burns stayed here while visiting Dundee. In 1854 the first telegraph office in Dundee was opened in the shop on the ground floor. The buildings on the opposite side of the street were erected in 1908–09 when the Cowgate was widened. Everything on the left has gone, having been flattened in the 1970s to make way for the Wellgate Centre.

Opposite: The Wishart Arch in Cowgate seen on a 1900s postcard. George Wishart (*c.*1513–1546) is believed to have been the younger brother of James Wishart of Pitarrow near Dundee. An early supporter of the Reformation, he lived abroad in self-imposed exile from 1538 to 1543. He returned to Pitarrow that year, but was forbidden from preaching by Cardinal Beaton. However, when plague struck Dundee the same year he preached courageously to the frightened townspeople, using the West Port as a pulpit. Three years later he was strangled and burned as a heretic in front of the Cardinal's castle in St Andrews. The gateway traditionally known as the Wishart Arch is probably a replacement, built during the strengthening of the town's defences in the 1590s. Visible through the arch is the John O' Groats pub, and above it the Wishart Memorial Church, erected in 1893. This church was attended by the young Mary Slessor.

This picture of the King's Theatre in Cowgate was probably taken shortly after it opened on 15 March 1909. The architect was Frank Thomson, son of Dundee's city engineer, and the building was designed at a distance, with plans sent to and from the city by post. The resulting drawings were based on an inaccurate site survey, but disaster was averted when Thomson's father pulled a few strings. He had a new public lavatory built which necessitated raising the road and pavement and was enough to compensate for the original error.

The interior of the King's was typically lavish for its period. In 1928 vaudeville succumbed to moving pictures and the theatre was converted into a cinema. Predictably, this closed in the 1970s and the King's became home to that very British form of gambling, bingo. The County Bingo, too, has now gone and the former theatre has been refurbished as an up-market bar.

Although the buildings in the right foreground have been replaced by unappealing glass and steel, much of St Andrew's Street as seen in this 1905 view has survived. The elegant spire of St Andrew's Church can be seen on the horizon. The two-storey building on the corner of the street in the middle distance is dated 1894.

The building peeping through the trees on the left of this 1907 picture of King Street was constructed in 1777 as a chapel for the Glasites. The sect was founded in 1730 by John Glas, who was deposed by the presbytery from his ministry at Tealing near Dundee for protesting about church politics. Glasites emphasised the need for Christian love and the voluntary nature of religion, and a bowl of broth was given to all worshippers at the end of each service, earning this the name the 'Kail Kirk'. The chapel was eventually sold to commercial concerns and the Glasites removed to their former soup kitchen to the rear. In 1928 this became the East Hall of St Andrew's Kirk. When this was to be demolished to make way for the inner ring road in 1973, the town compensated St Andrew's by giving it the former Glasite chapel, which remains a well-used hall for church and community activities. The tenements in the centre of the picture have been demolished and a car park for St Andrew's Church now occupies their site.

With the exception of the tower of St Mary's in the Nethergate, St Andrew's Parish Church is the oldest ecclesiastical building in Dundee. In the 1760s the population of the city was soaring. The provost and magistrates insisted that the entire populace must attend church on the Sabbath, but the capacity of the three City Churches had become woefully inadequate, and every Sunday some three or four thousand worshippers were denied access. Mary Queen of Scots had granted the lands of the former Greyfriars Monastery for the use of the town in 1564. These became the site of a cemetery and also the meeting place of members of the Nine Incorporated Trades of Dundee, hence the nickname 'The Howff'. Here they deliberated on the issues of the day, and in the mid-eighteenth century they quite logically came to the conclusion that Dundee had sore want of another kirk. The kirk session agreed, and a new church was planned. After the town council declined to make a contribution towards it, the church was funded by public subscription, the Incorporated and United Trades and the kirk session. Samuel Bell was chosen as architect and the foundation stone was laid in 1772, the church being completed in 1774. Until 1834 the so-called Trades' Kirk was a chapel of ease, subordinate to the established church, but in that year it became a parish church in its own right. Gas lighting replaced candlelight in the church in 1838, and the present stained glass was installed in 1892. One curiosity of this fine Georgian kirk is that it possesses a weather-vane in the form of a wyvern, believed to be unique in Scotland. This mythical creature is regarded as the guardian of treasure, appropriate to a church founded by men of trade and commerce.

ST ANDREWS PARISH

Opposite: The Wellgate Steps, or rather an approximation of them, were reinstated when the area was redeveloped. Everything else in this atmospheric 1909 view has gone. Ironically, at the time the Wellgate Centre was being upgraded and so many historic buildings and features were being destroyed, the traders' and council funded the restoration of the Victorian lamp standard at the top of the steps. Barefoot boys are a common enough sight in old photographs, but barefoot girls like the one in the left foreground much less so. This one appears to be holding out a cup in her right hand while the well-to-do trio opposite look the other way. The corner of Wellgate and Victoria Road was unique in Dundee in having two shops situated one above the other, both of which were at ground level. The lower shop, at 75 Wellgate, was occupied by Henderson & Co., house furnishers. The upper one, at 23 Victoria Road, was W. E. Dryden's well-known fruit shop.

In the early eighteenth century the Wellgate and Cowgate were fashionable middle class streets of merchants' houses. By the 1780s industry had begun to encroach on the area, notably thread-making, which was concentrated in the Wellgate, Seagate and Overgate and employed some 3,000 people around this date. An exodus of the wealthier citizens from this part of the city centre began in the mid-1830s, with those who could afford to do so moving out to the suburbs due to the pressures on living space and concerns about the spread of disease in the overcrowded city. This picture of the Wellgate was taken from Panmure Street in 1906.

The Victorian building in the left foreground of the upper picture was demolished to make way for the art deco premises of Claude Alexander. This popular Dundee tailor founded his business at 69 Murraygate in 1930 and transferred to his Wellgate/Panmure Street shop in 1936. Alexander's ceased trading in 1980 and the shop was demolished to make way for part of the mammoth Wellgate Centre, begun in 1977. Dundonians liked the old Wellgate; it had character and interesting wee shops. In today's Wellgate they can browse among chain stores to the strains of muzak, from which even the gents' offers no respite.

Opposite: In the mid-eighteenth century the Murraygate was a street of gentlemen's houses, described by a contemporary as being 'of moderate height and generally well built'. However, during the following century the backlands became cluttered with industrial premises and ramshackle slums, and by 1870 the Murraygate had become a ghetto of poverty, with one of the highest mortality rates in a city that had one of the highest in Britain. The slums were cleared under the powers of the 1871 Improvement Act and the Murraygate was widened and reinvented as a fashionable commercial thoroughfare. The skyline of this late 1920s view is now dominated by the Wellgate Centre.

Wellgate Steps. Dundee.

70340.JV.

This view, looking along Victoria Road, shows Dryden's shop on the right with Henderson's below it.

MURRAYGATE, DUNDEE

Dundee's La Scala cinema, third from the left, opened on 9 December 1913 and was the first custom-built picture house in the city. It was constructed for a Mr Ramsay Blair who owned a chain of some twenty cinemas. La Scala advertised afternoon tea served free of charge to patrons in the circle. Seats were priced at threepence, sixpence and one shilling. Private boxes for four could be obtained for five shillings – or seven and six for the best seats in the house.

The auditorium of La Scala photographed in 1913. In the era of silent movies the cinema's orchestra was conducted by Mr Routlege Bell. Newspaper accounts of the arrival of talking pictures in 1930 vary, some stating the orchestra was thrown out of work, while others say its musicians were retained and continued to play during the films and intervals. La Scala closed on 1 May 1965.

Potter's shoe shop, in the left foreground of this late 1920s view, was designed by Gauldie & Harris in 1911. Modified from an existing eighteenth century house, it is a rare example of the arts and crafts style in Dundee and merits a more appropriate contemporary shop-front. The tenement next door dates from 1783. The Murraygate marks the turning point in modern attitudes to development in Dundee. It is a quirky and pleasing mix of eighteenth century, Victorian, art deco and modern architecture, with ugly 1970s structures gradually being redeveloped or improved. Pedestrianisation, tramlines and cobbles provide ambience, and the street art, which in other cities is so often ponderous and inaccessible, is fun. My personal favourite is Tony Morrow's dragon.

William Spence's Clydesdale Bank of 1876 occupies the centre of this 1908 view of High Street, which still looks similar today. The facade was obscured by the handsome Georgian frontage of the Trades' Hall until this was demolished in 1878 to widen the street under the powers of the Improvement Act of the same year.

YOU KNOW THAT
KEILLER'S CELEBRATED DUNDEE MARMALADE
HAS OVER A CENTURY'S REPUTATION & IS STILL THE BEST.

NOW TRY
KEILLER'S
FINEST PRESERVES

WHICH ARE EQUALLY GOOD.
YOUR GROCER STOCKS THEM.

This rare advertising postcard dates from the early years of the last century and recalls one of Dundee's most famous companies. In 1797 one Janet Keiller and her son James ran a small business in the Seagate, manufacturing and selling confectionery and preserves. During the early 1840s the increasingly successful concern acquired additional premises at 1 Castle Street. This became a shop, while the original Seagate premises was turned into a factory. Quite when the family engaged in making marmalade is unknown, but they certainly did not invent it as some tales imply. It was a small part of the firm's manufacture until the 1850s and was at that time a coarse, sticky substance served as a desert. However, Alexander Keiller invented the thinner Scotch marmalade for spreading on bread and toast that we know today, and sales of the product soared. By 1860 a substantial factory had been built in Albert Square, and distinctive white Tyneside crocks had begun to be used as containers for the marmalade. This design classic is still in use today. The Keiller family's involvement with the firm ended in 1899, and in 1919 Keiller's merged with Crosse & Blackwell and Lazenbys. Expansion continued, with a new plant at Mains Loan opened in 1928 and a bakery in 1932. Further growth followed after 1945, when the manufacture of

Toblerone chocolate transferred to Dundee. A peak figure of 1,700 employees was reached in 1950. In 1961 Keiller's became part of the Nestlé group, and a decade later the Albert Square factory was closed with the loss of hundreds of jobs. It was demolished in 1978 and its site is now occupied by the Forum Centre (previously called the Keiller Centre). In 1988 the last Keiller factory in the city closed when marmalade production was transferred to Manchester.

As a footnote, there is an amusing anecdote about Keiller's in H. V. Morton's book *In Scotland Again* (1933). Morton visited the Dundee sweet factory, where he was told that Keiller's claimed the invention of 'Love Hearts' sweets. They were working on an up-to-date version called Cupid's Kisses, with inscriptions such as Say kid, I like your style; Gee but you're some baby; and You're a regular jazz hound. Morton enquired why Cupid had such an American accent, and was told the blocks used to print the mottoes were American.

'But do these sweets circulate in, say, Mull or Skye, or north of the Caledonian Canal?', quizzed Morton.

'No, they are only popular in towns which have cinemas.'

'In other words, towns which can translate them?'

'Yes.'

D. M. Brown's was one of Dundee's best-known draper's department stores, occupying huge premises at the corner of the High Street and Commercial Street. Founded in 1888, the business moved here in 1906, but it was not until 1908 that the corner premises occupied by the Maypole Dairy were acquired and a grand entrance to Brown's shopping arcade was developed. This was opened on 3 December the same year.

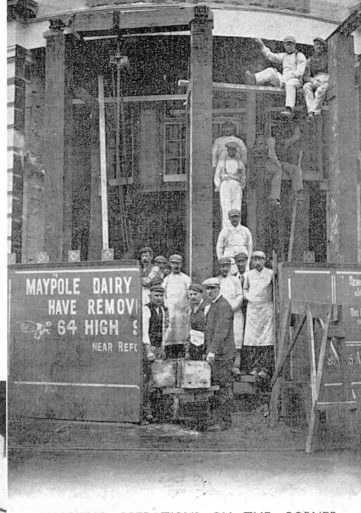

WORKING OPERATIONS ON THE CORNER
—— ENTRANCE TO THE ARCADE ——
At D. M. BROWN'S
:: :: :: DUNDEE :: :: ::

26th October 1908

Brown's was a fashionable place to take tea, where postcards, overprinted on the reverse with the legend 'Meet me in the Arcade', were provided gratis. Latterly D. M. Brown's became part of the Scottish Drapery Corporation Ltd., and in 1952 the company was acquired by House of Fraser.

Opening of the Arcade at D. M. BROWN'S, 80 High Street, Dundee   'Meet me in the Arcade.'

41

The Imperial Billiard Saloon occupies premises above the Maypole Dairy and Timpson's shoe shop on the left of this 1950 view of High Street. Next door at street level there was a branch of Keiller's confectioners, beside which a vennel known as New Inn Entry led to their chocolate factory in Albert Square, from which the alluring aroma would emerge and give Dundonians 'a notion'. The lower building to the right is the last surviving example of an early eighteenth century merchant's house on the High Street, while behind the street frontage is Gardyne's land, a property dating back to c.1600. The oldest building in the city centre, it is currently the subject of an ambitious restoration.

Opposite: The Royal British Hotel was erected in 1842 at the corner of High Street and Castle Street. In recent years it became Dundee University's Chalmers hall of residence, but this has now closed and the former hotel is presently unoccupied.

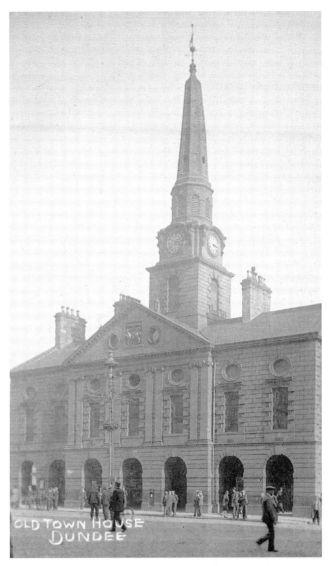

Dundee Town House dated from 1731, although the clock in the tower bore the year 1735. It was the work of the renowned Scottish architect William Adam (1689–1748) father of John (1721–92) and Robert Adam (1728–92), a trio whose neoclassical style came to typify an age, not just in Scotland but also south of the border. In the late nineteenth century the council chamber was adorned with a set of stained glass windows designed by Edward Burne-Jones and executed by William Morris & Co., depicting characters from Dundee's history. Despite these symbols of civic pride, it was felt the Town House had become too small for the city's status, and in 1911 James Thomson designed a new civic centre on the site of the Earl Grey Dock. The American influence in Thomson's taste was reflected in the plan, which resembled the Capitol building in Washington DC. This was never carried through, but in 1912 a donation from the jute magnate Sir James Key Caird for a new town hall was to seal the fate of the Town House, which was demolished to make way for its successor

The old Town House, known affectionately to generations of locals as 'The Pillars', is on the right of this 1907 picture. Clearance work for the new municipal buildings began in 1913, sweeping away such treasures as the seventeenth century burgh weigh house and grammar school to the rear of the Town House. The Caird Hall was completed on the site in 1922. When City Square was designed in 1924 by Sir John Burnet, it was suggested that the old Town House could perhaps remain in situ or be moved and re-erected at the west end of the High Street. In the end it was unemployment which was the deciding factor: the destruction of the old Town House in 1931 provided much-needed jobs at a time of recession.

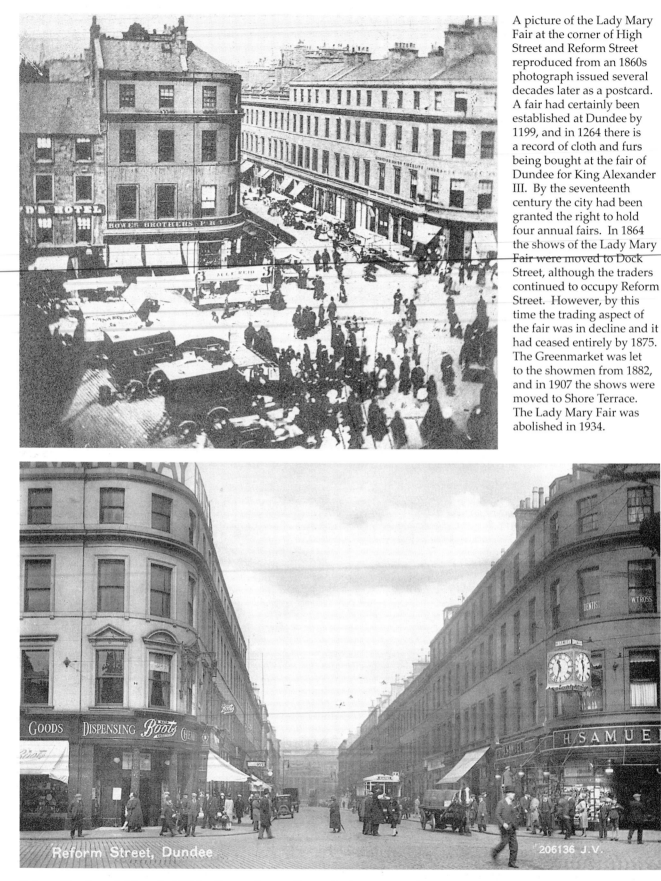

A picture of the Lady Mary Fair at the corner of High Street and Reform Street reproduced from an 1860s photograph issued several decades later as a postcard. A fair had certainly been established at Dundee by 1199, and in 1264 there is a record of cloth and furs being bought at the fair of Dundee for King Alexander III. By the seventeenth century the city had been granted the right to hold four annual fairs. In 1864 the shows of the Lady Mary Fair were moved to Dock Street, although the traders continued to occupy Reform Street. However, by this time the trading aspect of the fair was in decline and it had ceased entirely by 1875. The Greenmarket was let to the showmen from 1882, and in 1907 the shows were moved to Shore Terrace. The Lady Mary Fair was abolished in 1934.

Reform Street was laid out in 1832 by George Angus. It was the first street to be constructed to plans set out by William Burn in 1824 for the improvement of the city. The High School facing into the street is also by George Angus and opened in 1834, the foundation stone having been laid in 1832. Reform Street is the most classically elegant in the city centre and remains pleasingly familiar from this 1929 view.

We ARE COMING Thursday.
TO SEE YOU SOON

A·CAIRD&·SONS·
·OUTFITTERS·
·DUNDEE·

The expressions on the faces of Alexander Caird and his son, also called Alexander, make the message on this postcard seem like a threat! Caird entered business in 1879 as a travelling vendor of drapery goods, known as a 'farandman'. From his first forays into the Carse of Gowrie, he earned a reputation for quality as far afield as the Braes of Mar. He opened his first shop in Union Street in 1901, moving to larger premises in Reform Street in 1915 and subsequently opening branches in Perth, St Andrews and Elgin. The prestigious Dundee store closed in the 1970s.

This picture dates from around 1910 and depicts 'The Hub', which was styled Dundee's smallest shop. It was located at 63 High Street, next door to Samuel's the jewellers on the corner of Reform Street. When this picture was taken it was owned by William Young, tobacconist. In later years it was run by the Lamb family.

Both these illustrations show the building at the corner of High Street and Overgate known as General Monck's Lodging. The upper one dates from 1920 and the lower one was taken in 1951. It was here that General Monck stayed after the capture of Dundee by Cromwell's forces in 1651. The house dated from the fifteenth century and once had a row of arches on the ground floor which led to shops set back from the street. In old Scots these were known as luckens and earned the building the name of the Luckenbooth. The stair tower rising above the top of the building was once a commonplace sight in Dundee, and was a consequence of merchants' houses being reduced in height after the sack of the city by Monck's troops, since their owners could not afford to repair the damage caused by the arson of the Roundheads. All these buildings were demolished in 1964 to make way for the second phase of the Overgate Centre.

Opposite: The Overgate looking towards St Paul's Cathedral in 1904. The popular Dundee tearoom, Franchi's, was located in the third building from the left. The orgy of destruction which preceded the development of the Overgate began in 1956 with the digging of a massive hole for the foundations of the Angus Hotel, although the buildings in this view survived until 1964. At the time of their demolition a council spokesman wrote: 'Buildings here heard the tramp of English soldiers intent on the town's surrender. Today it is the clank of bulldozers and the crash of ancient masonry as a way is cleared for 1964's geometric lines. On the new rooftops will be car parks.'

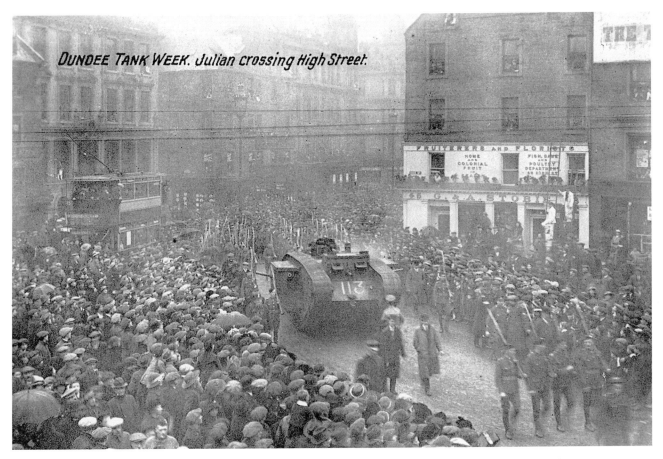

In the closing months of the First World War the tank *Julian* toured Britain. The exercise had two purposes: to let the public see the new technology being employed at the front, and to encourage them to buy War Bonds to help with the war effort. When *Julian* visited Dundee in February 1918 the week-long drive raised £4.5 million, an amazing sum for the time.

This 1907 photograph was taken outside Andrew Birrell & Sons bootmakers and shows the intersection of the Overgate and Lindsay Street. During the destruction of the Overgate some 2,700 pottery fragments were uncovered, some dating back to the thirteenth century. It is to be much regretted that the deep foundations of the Overgate development destroyed for ever so much of the potential archaeology of the town centre. The picture to the right shows a closer view of Birrell's well-known shop.

Dolls, gramophones, crockery, jeely pans and an old bedstead are among the motley selection of articles on offer in this picture of the Mid Kirk Style, taken in May 1950. This vennel ran between South Lindsay Street and Tally Street, with the high wall on the left at the back of the City Churches site. The weekly Saturday markets ceased when the area was cleared in 1957.

Opposite: This picture of the junction of the Overgate and South Lindsay Street in May 1956 shows demolition of the area already well underway. Next door to the doomed ancient house with its gable to the camera was the Mercat Cross bar, owned at the time by William Hutchison, one-time chairman of Dundee United FC. On the left was J. B. Lawson's, noted as the only pub in the city to have three entrances. Lawson's was founded between 1862 and 1864, and in the 1890s its owner acquired warehouses in Seagate and began a wholesale whisky export business. Both these popular watering holes were closed and pulled down in 1957.

Whitehall Street, Dundee.

WILMAR SERIES.

A view of Whitehall Street looking towards the Nethergate in 1904 and affording a glimpse of Thorter Row beyond (thorter is an old Scots word for a crossing). This narrow street was reputed to be the shortest in Dundee, and contained the popular Cafe Royal bar. Established in 1845 and listed as a hotel in 1864 and a restaurant by 1900, the Cafe Royal was latterly owned by George D. Henderson, who played for Rangers before signing with Dundee United. Thomas Justice & Sons, whose shop can be seen in the left foreground, continued to trade from this site into the 1970s. The premises of Wm. Kidd & Son, printers, were situated beyond Justice's.

Opposite: Whitehall Street and Crescent were constructed during the years 1885–89 on the site of what had previously been one of the filthiest slum quarters in the city. The buildings were built for William Kidd, a Dundee publisher, to plans drawn up by Robert Keith. Considering he was a mason and not an architect by profession, his Gothic elegance wasn't a bad first effort! At the time this 1920s picture was taken, much of the west side of the street was occupied by Draffen's, established in 1887 and another of Dundee's huge drapery stores, which had a stylish tearoom 'panelled like an ocean liner'.

Permanent waving by the Eugene process ensures to the patron permanent satisfaction. It is the only process used in the hairdressing section at DRAFFEN'S

CHILDREN'S HAIRDRESSING – AN ART IN ITSELF – IS PRACTICED WITH COMPLETE SUCCESS IN DRAFFEN'S HAIRDRESSING DEPT.

Above: Advertising postcards for Draffen's hairdressing department, dating from the early 1930s. The little girl's hair is very like that of the infant Princess Elizabeth in a contemporary photograph. Incorporated as Draffen & Jarvie in 1910, the company became Draffens of Dundee in 1948 and was subsequently acquired by Grants (East of Scotland) Ltd., before being taken over by Debenhams in the 1970s. By this time they had acquired both Kidd's and Justice's premises, and with the exception of the upper floors of 11 Whitehall Street (which belonged to Thorntons, solicitors) owned the whole of the west side of Whitehall Street. Debenhams closed the store when they moved into the new Overgate Centre in 2000.

Rev Walter Walsh

Gilfillan Memorial Church Dundee

J.B.W. D.

The Gilfillan Memorial Church was designed by James Stark and erected in 1887. Gilfillan was an outspoken social reformer and numbered among the patrons of William MacGonagall (doggerel poet). The Revd Walter Walsh, inset, was a member of the Prohibition Party and also played a significant part in the setting up of the Jute and Flax Workers' Union, established in 1906. This Edwardian postcard is one of a series of over twenty pictures of Dundee churches and their incumbents published by J. B. White of the Nethergate. Issued around 1908, they were among the first cards published by the firm, notable for their large output of Scottish views from the 1930s to 1950s. Now trading as Whiteholme Ltd., this family-owned business still includes postcards among its wide range of products, which also features greetings cards and stationery. Whiteholme Ltd. are Britain's oldest surviving postcard publishers.

The premises of Pettie & Whitelaw, surgical instrument manufacturers, at 96 Nethergate. The business was established between 1900 and 1903 at 43 Commercial Street, transferring to this shop in 1907, at which time they were described as limb, bandage and truss manufacturers to Dundee Royal Infirmary. In 1911 the business moved to 128 Nethergate, becoming Pettie & Co. in 1913. The shop closed in 1957.

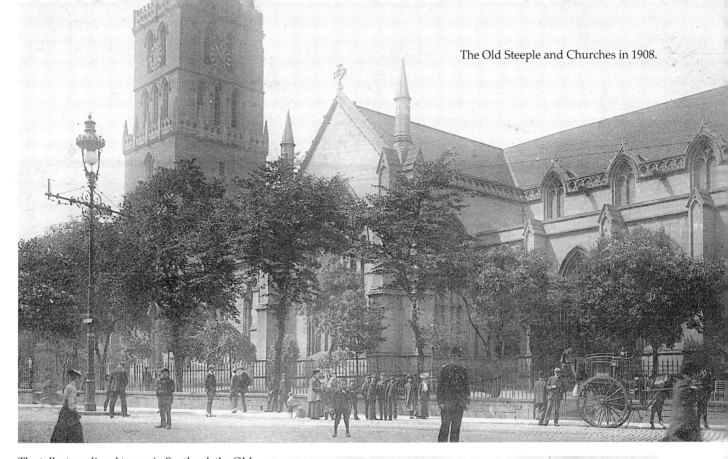

The Old Steeple and Churches in 1908.

The tallest medieval tower in Scotland, the Old Steeple was erected some time between 1460 and 1500 and was part of a rebuilding of the original St Mary's Church, founded around 1190 and destroyed by Edward I in 1303. Both the nave (adjacent to the tower) and the steeple were burned by English soldiers in 1548 when they sacked the church and carried off the bells. Although the steeple was subsequently repaired, the nave remained in ruins and was used as a quarry. After the Reformation in 1560 the building was divided into three smaller churches; further indignities were heaped upon it by the forces of General Monck in 1651. Tradition maintains that when Dundee welcomed the Old Pretender in 1715, the bells were rung with such vigour that they cracked. The present Steeple Church was designed by Samuel Bell and erected in 1787 on the site of the destroyed nave. Until then the steeple had been free-standing for over 200 years. In 1841 fire destroyed much of the church, and although the architect William Burn pronounced it saveable, a slump in the building trade was the reason for its demolition. Burn designed the replacement, completed in 1847.

Opposite: Church Lane can be see branching off on the right of this early 1950s picture of Nethergate. All the buildings on this side of the street were removed to build the Overgate Centre, which was completed in 1964. Nethergate was formerly known as Flukergate, from fluke, the Scots word for a flounder, this being the site of Dundee's medieval fish market.

The Old Steeple viewed from South Lindsay Street in 1934.

OLD STEEPLE, DUNDEE.   A.231.

53

South Lindsay Street, seen here in 1955, was built partly on the site of the Corbie Hill, which had been erased by quarrying by the 1860s. The shows of the Lady Mary Fair were located in the disused quarry for a brief period before they were relocated to Dock Street in 1864. This broad and well-built street was another casualty of the redevelopment of the Overgate.

In the late thirteenth century Dundee's Mercat Cross was located in the Seagate, the heart of the city at that time. It was probably moved to the Marketgate (High Street) in the second half of the fourteenth century. A new Mercat Cross was built by the mason John Mylne in 1586. The shaft, capped with a unicorn, stood upon an octagonal castellated plinth atop a flight of steps. In 1777 the city fathers had it removed from the west end of the High Street as it had become an obstruction to traffic, and in 1874 the shaft was re-erected on a new plinth in the Nethergate and capped with a replacement unicorn sculpted by Scott Sutherland RSA. Russell's Royal Hotel, in the centre of this 1930s view, opened in 1839. After lying unoccupied for some years it was converted to flats in 1992.

The building second from the right in this early 1930s view was built in 1929 as Draffen's men's department. Beyond is the recently completed City Square. The Caird Hall was designed by James Thomson, and the foundation stone was laid by King George V in 1914. It was formally opened by his son, Edward, Prince of Wales. City Square was designed by Sir John Burnet in 1931 and opened by George, Duke of Kent on 30 November 1933.

It was the late fifteenth century before buildings in the Nethergate extended much beyond St Mary's Church. Before then only a few prestigious houses stood in this part of the city, notably the twelfth century mansion of Earl David, which is believed to have stood opposite the church.

55

Green's magnificent Playhouse cinema opened its doors on 4 March 1936. It was designed by John Fairweather, but Green imported Joseph Emberton from Blackpool as second architect and it was he who gave the building its contemporary art deco style. With seating for 4,117 people it was at the time one of the largest cinemas in Britain. In the centre of the picture is one of Andrew G. Kidd's delivery vans, painted in red and showing a baker holding a loaf. This well-known firm of bakers and confectioners had their office and bakery at 5 Lytton Street, plus several shops around the city.

NETHERGATE, DUNDEE.

GREEN'S PLAYHOUSE, NETHERGATE, DUNDEE.   A.3694.

When illuminated, Emberton's glass, steel and concrete advertising tower could be seen from miles around. Green's also contained a fashionable restaurant with 160 seats, and the capacity of this was doubled on Sundays when additional tables took over the foyer (this was only possible because film showings were prohibited on Sundays). The cinema's interior was sumptuously furnished, with screen curtains made from satin and silk, velvet upholstery and extensive use of marble.

Opposite: Green's lavish, gilded auditorium was designed by John Alexander of Newcastle and reflected contemporary American style – not that the many Dundonians who sampled the first innocent fumblings of romance in the back row cared! The Playhouse was converted into a Mecca bingo hall, reckoned to be the biggest such establishment in the world, and what remained of Green's interior was destroyed by a disastrous fire in 1995. The tower faced an uncertain fate but was retained when the Mecca bingo was rebuilt.

THE MAIN ENTRANCE TO CAFÉ & THEATRE, GREEN'S PLAYHOUSE, NETHERGATE, DUNDEE.

Cinema attendances fell right across Britain during the 1960s. Television is usually cited as the cause, but many households were still without a set by 1970. It was probably the British film industry itself which was to blame. The public had lapped up a diet of jingoism in wartime, and the feel-good Ealing comedies of the 1950s. In the 1960s writers and directors began producing gritty 'kitchen sink' dramas, or artily shot romps with unfathomable endings. Ironically, much of the cinema of this period has achieved cult status, but in its day people who lived in poverty in crumbling tenements did not want to see their lives mirrored on the silver screen. Many decried 1960s cinema with the phrase 'Hooray, we're a' daft'. Green's closed its doors in 1970.

GENERAL VIEW OF STAGE & PROSCENIUM, GREENS PLAYHOUSE, NETHERGATE, DUNDEE.

From art deco elegance to 1960s brutalism in the turn of a page. This postcard shows the recently completed Angus Hotel, the first phase of the Overgate redevelopment, which opened in 1964. One of its first functions was to host a dinner for the centenary of the granting of a royal charter to Dundee Chamber of Commerce. It was a prestigious building, finished in granite, marble and Norwegian quartz, but by the 1990s its appearance was hopelessly dated. It was demolished in 2000 and Debenham's new store now occupies the site.

The inner ring road now rushes across the foreground of the Nethergate as seen in this 1907 view looking towards Perth Road. In 1821 this was a fashionable part of town and detached Georgian villas belonging to the gentry ranked along the left-hand side of the street. The finialled Gothic twin towers on the right belonged to St Enoch's Church, which was built in 1875. Demolished in 1961, its site is now taken by the Bank of Scotland.

The *Courier* building in Meadowside Road was designed in an American-inspired style by Niven & Wiggleworth and built in 1902; this picture was taken a few years after its completion. In 1960 the adjoining tower of offices was added. The *Dundee Advertiser* was founded in 1801 and the *Courier* in 1816. In 1866 the *Advertiser* was bought by John Leng, and in 1886 the shipping magnate William Thomson acquired the *Courier*. Thomson had been whittling away at Leng's Bank Street empire for some years, and when he died in 1906 D. C. Thomson & Co. took over his remaining publishing interests. The company currently employs around 3,000.

The Albert Institute was funded by the Baxters and other Dundee manufacturers as a memorial to Prince Albert. Initial plans were prepared in 1865–67 by the celebrated architect George Gilbert Scott, the central portion being added in 1873 and the eastern galleries in 1887. Following its renovation in 1983 it was renamed in honour of Lord Provost Maurice McManus. Queen Victoria, with her back determinedly to the building, would not have been amused.

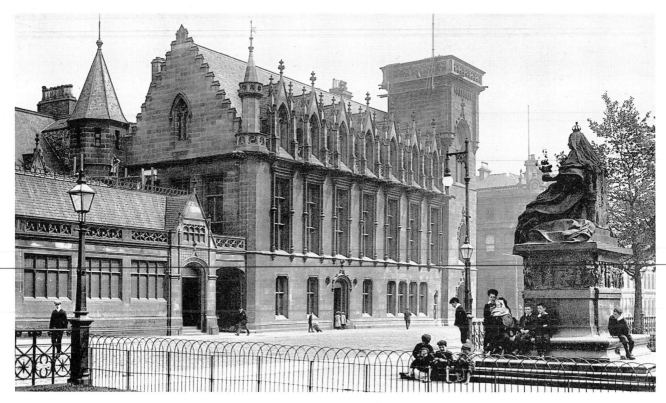

The Royal Exchange was designed in 1854–55 by David Bryce for the Dundee Chamber of Commerce as a replacement for their old meeting place, the Baltic Coffee House in the Cowgate. The original plans included a splendid spire, but it was decided after construction had begun that the site chosen was too marshy and the ground would not support its weight. The low Gothic building on the left of this 1908 view was the Jute Shelter, added a few years later, where the jute barons would transact their business. This was demolished and replaced by the Guardian Royal Exchange building in 1957, a rare proof in Dundee that 1950s architecture didn't always have to be bad.

Bluejackets from the submarine tender *Vulcan* march past the Royal Exchange on the occasion of the funeral of King Edward VII in May 1910. Crosses on postcards like this usually indicate 'this is me', but poignantly the message on the back of the card explains that this young seaman was drowned a couple of weeks later.

Constitution Road in 1905 showing the YMCA building second from the right and beyond it Dundee Congregational Church. This opened in 1833 as the Independent Church of Dundee, becoming known as Ward Chapel. The building in the foreground now houses the Regional Music Centre, but was built in 1840 as the Bell Street United Presbyterian Church, whose congregation was dissolved in 1940. The basement of the church was a popular venue for entertainments, and on 2 January 1865 was hosting Springthorpe's promenade concerts. A large crowd had gathered outside, and as people were descending the icy steps a group surged forward and there was a tremendous crush. Twenty lives were lost, among them those of several children.

The Sheriff Court House was built in 1833–34 to a design by George Angus and William Scott, with the original plans including a much larger complex of buildings than was finally executed. The prison, largely obscured by the court house in this 1905 postcard view, was also completed in 1834, and received its first inmates in 1837. It was extended in the 1860s and remained the burgh gaol until 1927. The gaol site

was taken over by the Corporation Transport Department which extended the tram depot adjacent to the prison to form a new central depot for both buses and trams, with work beginning in 1929. It was housing only buses by 1972 when it was vacated to make way for part of the inner ring road and police headquarters. The building in the background of the view was Tay Works, owned by Gilroy Bros. and once described as the longest jute factory in the world. It has now been converted to flats.

In 1746 Dundee had no effective means of dealing with fires and 'houses burnt at their leisure'. By 1775 the city had two 'water engines' and by the early nineteenth century two fire insurance companies who operated pumps. After lengthy discussions the city fathers inaugurated a fire establishment under municipal control in 1835. This view shows part of the new central fire station, which opened in 1900 in West Bell Street, the same year the city received its first steam fire engine. Both this picture and the one below feature Captain James Weir, who served as Dundee's firemaster from 1903 to 1937. He is standing on the left in this view, and is seated next to the driver of the right-hand appliance in the lower picture.

This view shows the whole of the fire station and dates from after 1911, the year in which the city introduced its first motor engine (this is the vehicle on the right, an Argyll). The last of the horses were sold off in 1917. In 1970 the West Bell Street station was closed and the brigade moved to new premises in Blackness Road. The old building was subsequently demolished. The brigades of Angus, Perthshire and Kinross were amalgamated to form Tayside Fire Brigade in 1975.

Central Fire Brigade Station, Dundee.

Although strictly speaking the Queen's Hotel belongs in the city centre section of this book, the inner ring road has so effectively cut off the section of the Nethergate in which it stands that it is now more a part of Perth Road than the Nethergate. The Queen's was built in 1878 and designed by Young & Meldrum in a Gothic-meets-Second Empire style. Tradition says its site was chosen because the proprietor had been told that it would be right beside the rail terminus for the Tay Bridge, and was later to discover he had been misinformed. The dinner for the launch of the *Discovery* was held here in 1901, and the original menu was recreated for its centenary.

The Caird Rest opened in 1912 as a centre for 'rest and recreation' for elderly Dundonians, and was in essence a forerunner of today's day centres. It was one of the many benefactions of James Key Caird (1837–1914) of the Ashton Jute Works. His other gifts to Dundee include Camperdown House and Park, the Caird Hall and Park, and generous donations to Dundee Royal Infirmary. The Rest is now the university department of applied language studies.

A donation of £120,000 by Dr John Boyd Baxter and Miss Mary Ann Baxter led to the founding of Dundee's University College in 1881. This occupied the four Georgian villas in the foreground of this 1912 picture. University College Dundee became part of St Andrews University in 1897 and was renamed Queen's College Dundee in 1954 when it was incorporated with the Medical School. It bore this name until becoming the University of Dundee on 1 August 1967.

Left and below: Students take part in rag week celebrations outside Queen's College in the early 1950s. The Georgian villas which had been the college's original home were unsentimentally pulled down to make way for the 1959 tower by Sir Robert Matthew, and from modest beginnings the university has now subsumed much of the east end of Perth Road. Looking at concrete monstrosities such as Belmont Hall (1963) and the medical sciences building (1970), one is left musing on the perversity that Britain's universities, seats of culture and learning, have consistently imposed some of the ugliest structures imaginable on our townscapes.

Opposite top: James Aitken's grocery and vintners premises at the corner of Perth Road and Miller's Wynd, pictured around 1885. Note that over the years the eighteenth century building has undergone a series of upgradings. The part facing the camera has been heightened and a wooden stair added, probably to create a new entrance when the shop frontage was built. This wooden staircase is about to be superseded by a curved stair tower, on the left, which is in the process of construction. The labour and expense was, alas, wasted as the building was pulled down and replaced by a row of tenements in the 1890s.

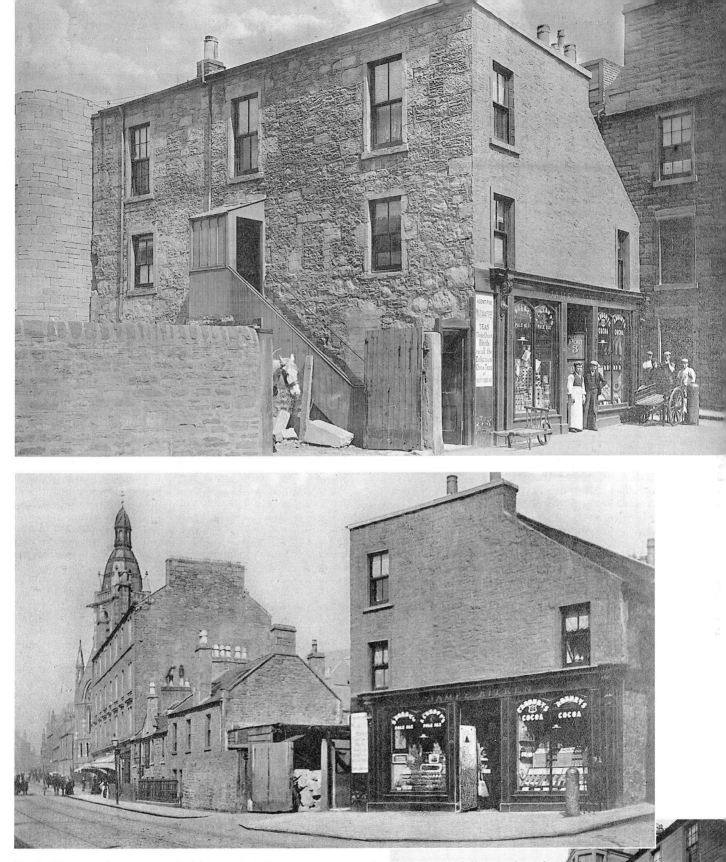

The buildings in the foreground of this picture all appear on a map of 1821 on which Miller's Wynd is marked as East Wynd. At that time this area was near the western extremity of the city at the Sinderins. The family business founded by James Aitken in 1874 still trades from the exact same corner today, on the ground floor of the tenement which rose on the site of the original building. Ryehill Church, which opened in 1878, can be seen in the background. This was converted into flats in 1987.

This view shows, on the right, the tenement in Perth Road where Aitken's shop is located.

Blackness library was designed in 1904 by Frank Thomson, son of city engineer James Thomson. The site was a gift from Sir John Roberston of Elmslea and the library was formally opened on 22 October 1908. Construction was aided by a donation of £7,000 from the Carnegie Trust. It is a sad reflection on the times in which we live that it now requires a security guard.

Blackness Avenue, pictured here around 1910, follows the course of the driveway which once led to Blackness House. This picturesque and substantial seventeenth century manor house was demolished in the 1930s. The first two buildings on the right were erected in 1868 and designed by James Maclaren. The adjacent tenement, dated 1870, must be the most optimistically named in all Dundee – Viewforth Terrace!

Blackness Terrace in 1903. When first built these middle-class tenements lay close to the edge of the city. From 1850 onwards several exclusive villas were erected beyond them, and this type of housing continued to characterise the development of the area into the 1930s. The continuation of Perth Road is like a catalogue of architectural history, with styles ranging from baronial, through art nouveau and arts and crafts to art deco.

Buffalo Bill's Wild West Show arrived on Magdalen Green on 12 August 1904 towards the end of its two year tour of Britain. Among the attractions were bronco busting, horseback stunt riding, trick shooting, and huge staged battles with Red Indians (Native Americans, if you please!), among them Chief Red Shirt, who would lead an attack on the Deadwood Stage. In all some 600 men and 500 horses were involved, and the staging of the show, which thrilled audiences in 134 towns and cities, was a massive logistical task.

Magdalen Green is supposed to derive its name from a medieval nunnery dedicated to St Mary Magdalen which stood in the vicinity. During the early nineteenth century Magdalen Green Yard was the site of a number of large political meetings. In 1819 George Kinloch, dubbed the radical laird, addressed a large assembly with a speech on the need for parliamentary reform. In 1832 the site hosted a gathering of those supporting the Dundee Political Union, another pro-reform party. Ten years later it was the gathering point for 4,000 people who were to march to Forfar for the Chartist cause. Despite alarm among the people of Forfar, the march ended with some 400 hungry, weary souls limping dejectedly into the town in the small hours.

To relieve unemployment during a period of deep recession, some twenty acres of Magdalen Green were laid out in the early 1840s as Dundee's first public park. A bandstand was added in 1889 and has recently been restored.

The first part of the Dundee & Newtyle Railway opened from Law station on 16 February 1831, and the first locomotive ran to Newtyle in 1833. Magdalen Green station, seen here in 1905, opened in 1845 and was closed in 1956.

A peaceful view of the cobbled Esplanade on a sunny day in the early 1920s. The street was constructed on reclaimed land and was completed as far as the landfall of the anticipated Tay Rail Bridge in 1875, after which it continued westward in stages during the 1880s. In 1888, however, a proposed continuation of the road as far as Windsor Street was decided against, with a footbridge (shown in the upper picture) over the railway at Magdalen Green being the inexpensive alternative.

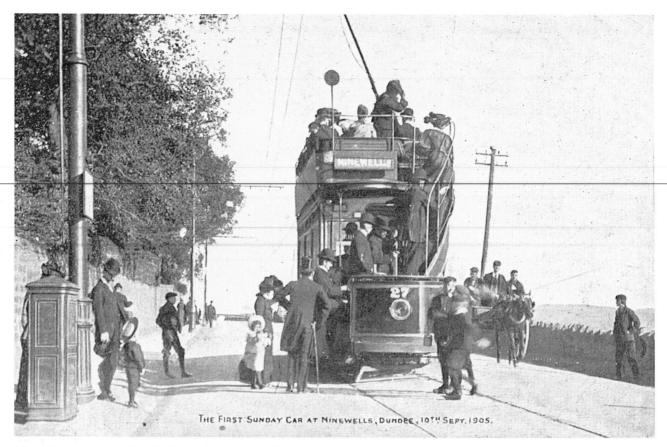

THE FIRST SUNDAY CAR AT NINEWELLS, DUNDEE, 10TH SEPT. 1905.

Now a busy artery to Dundee's western suburbs, the Perth Road at Ninewells was once in a rural setting. Pleasure seekers escaping the city disembarked at the tram stop here, and this stretch of the Tay was a popular bathing place. The picture on this postcard view dates from 10 September 1905, the occasion of the running of Dundee's first Sunday tramcars.

Another Edwardian view of rural Ninewells, this time depicting the joinery premises of Thomas Hay & Sons. The business was founded in 1878 but was given up in 1925. Here the workforce are posing with a roof cruck (support), perhaps bound for a barn in the nearby Carse of Gowrie.

Ninewells Joinery, Dundee.

The Hawkhill seen from the West Port in 1907. Situated beyond the city boundary, the Hawkhill was where travelling pedlars (known since the fifteenth century as hawkers) and itinerant labourers could ply their wares or services. Brook Street (on the right in this picture) continued as Milnbank Road and was obliterated in the early 1960s to make way for the inner ring road. On a map of 1821 these streets appear as Witch Loan and Scouring Burn respectively. The Globe Tavern, behind the tram, was built in 1823 and its clock is dated 1864. In 1980 the building was derelict, but it is now once again a popular rendezvous.

Prior to the passing of the 1872 Dundee Improvement Act the backlands of the city centre became filled with an ever more oppressive and unregulated clutter of slums and industrial premises. This 1900s view shows Small's Close at 6 Hawkhill and illustrates just how bad some of the housing conditions were. It was not until 1929 that the Hawkhill was the subject of a major slum clearance programme.

71

Not a stone of this 1920s view of Hawkhill looking back towards the city survives. In its place a wide band of asphalt is edged with featureless verges and overshadowed by concrete and steel. In the right foreground is a branch of the Dundee Eastern Co-operative Society. Founded in 1873, by 1900 the society had seventeen branches and its own bakery in West Clepington Road. There were four branches in Hawkhill alone: a bakery at No. 115; grocery at No. 153; drapers at No. 84; and bootmakers at No. 82.

Dundee Eastern Co-op's branch at 153 Hawkhill, *c.*1910. The society was absorbed into the Co-op chain of supermarkets in the 1970s, and most of the small branch stores which survived the bulldozers at that time have since been closed.

Another view of the Hawkhill, seen from further west than the picture on the facing page and taken on a clear day in 1907. Late eighteenth century buildings are distinguishable from those built from 1850 onwards by the fact that the newer tenements are taller. Again not a stone remains, and it is only topography and memory which makes it possible to accurately place the view.

Hawkhill, looking West

Some bits and pieces have survived to locate this 1907 picture looking toward the Sinderins, or 'sunderance' (dividing point), where the Perth Road and Hawkhill either meet or part with one another, depending on your point of view. Hawkhill School was designed by J. H. Langlands in 1892.

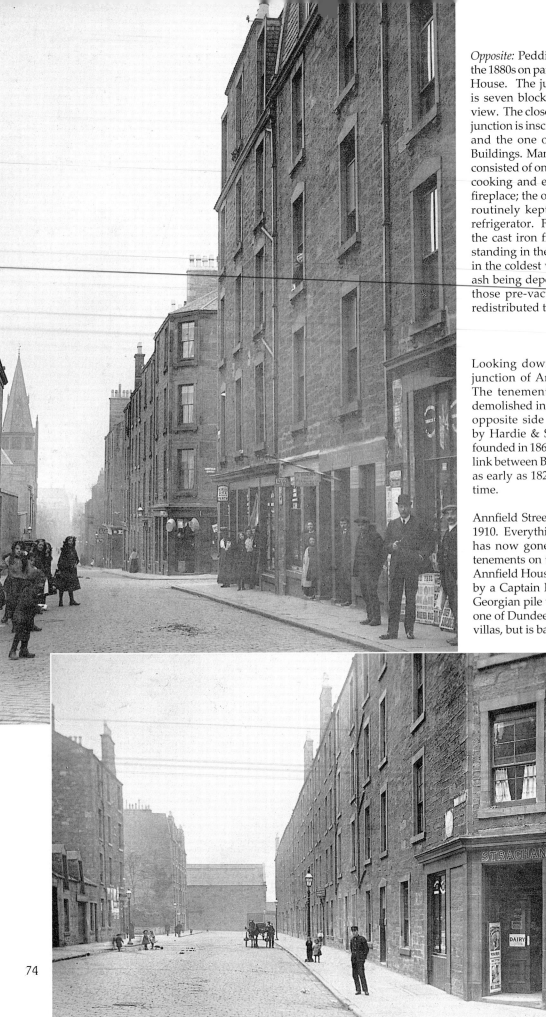

Opposite: Peddie Street was developed from the 1880s on part of the grounds of Blackness House. The junction of Abbotsford Place is seven blocks from the left of this 1907 view. The close on Peddie Street before this junction is inscribed Washington Buildings, and the one on the other side Waverley Buildings. Many of Dundee's tenement flats consisted of only two rooms: one for living, cooking and eating in which contained a fireplace; the other a dormitory which was routinely kept cold so as to double as a refrigerator. Few had a built-in grate and the cast iron fire basket was usually free-standing in the fireplace. This was lit only in the coldest weather as it led to a film of ash being deposited all over the room. In those pre-vacuum days, dusting merely redistributed the ash!

Looking down Annfield Road, with the junction of Annfield Street on the right. The tenements in the foreground were demolished in the 1970s. The whole of the opposite side of the street was occupied by Hardie & Smith's Baltic Linen Works, founded in 1864. Annfield Road existed as a link between Blackness Road and Hawkhill as early as 1821, but was unnamed at that time.

Annfield Street seen from Peddie Street in 1910. Everything on the right of the picture has now gone. The break in the line of tenements on the left marks the location of Annfield House, built in 1793 and occupied by a Captain McKenzie in 1821. This fine Georgian pile with its curved central bay is one of Dundee's oldest surviving suburban villas, but is badly in need of restoration.

Looking up Peddie Street from Hawkhill in 1910. The right-hand side of the street has been cleared, but the buildings on the left have been stone-cleaned and refurbished. Most tenement floors were covered with waxcloth and patterned linoleum was considered upmarket. Cooking was usually done on a simple gas appliance known as 'the Main', but some households made do with a gas ring placed on a box, on which precarious pots of washing might also be boiled. Light, too, was provided by gas and many Dundee homes did not have electricity installed until the 1950s.

75

Logie Central School on Blackness Road opened in 1928 and was designed by G. C. Soutar. It was built to provide three to four year vocational courses for children considered less literate than their peers. In 1976 it became the junior pupils' annexe of Harris Academy but closed several years ago. The empty building was set alight by vandals in March 2001 and has since been demolished.

Rosefield Street looks much the same as it did when this 1910 view was taken, but the close at number 19 on the right has been rebuilt in brick, evidence of tragic events which unfolded on the night of 5 November 1940 when a German bomb smashed into the tenement, blowing out the walls and causing the complete collapse of the roof and interior. Eleven people were pulled alive from the rubble, but Mrs Mary Laing and Robert Coventry were killed. Another bomb which destroyed 13 Briarwood Terrace during the same raid claimed the life of Mrs Elizabeth Cooper. Of 38 bombs which fell on Dundee from 1940 to 1943, these were the only fatalities.

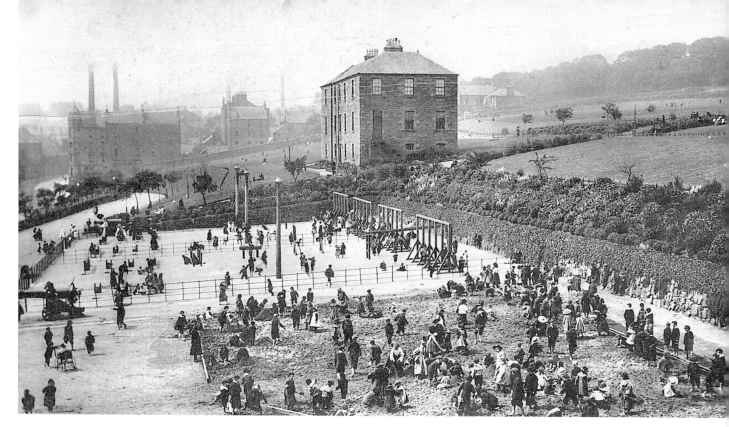

Dudhope Bank, in the centre of this 1908 view, was built in the 1870s as the Dundee Institution for the Education of the Deaf. It was funded by Mr Drysdale, who had worked with the organisation since its foundation in the 1840s. Dudhope Castle and its grounds were bought by the town council and laid out as a public park in 1893. The castle dates from 1580 and was built for the Scrymgeours, hereditary constables of Dundee. After years of neglect and use as a woollen mill, barracks and storehouse, it was restored in 1989.

Dundee Royal Infirmary was founded in 1798 in King Street, and initially patients would only receive treatment if they were a subscriber or referred by a subscriber. The infirmary moved to Barrack Street in 1855, occupying an Elizabethan-style pile designed by architects Coe & Goodwin. The nurses' home stood apart from the main building, and is shown here in 1910 with a polychrome brick extension. Parents were allowed to visit for only one hour a week, and since they were only admitted when that hour had started part of it was spent traversing the corridors. Parents of children not expected to live were given a white card which entitled them to unlimited visits.

MATERNITY DEPARTMENT, DUNDEE ROYAL INFIRMARY.

The maternity department at DRI was paid for by a donation by James Key Caird. Until the setting up of the National Health Service in 1948, the infirmary was still partly dependant on public subscriptions and this postcard comes from a long series published in 1925 to raise funds.

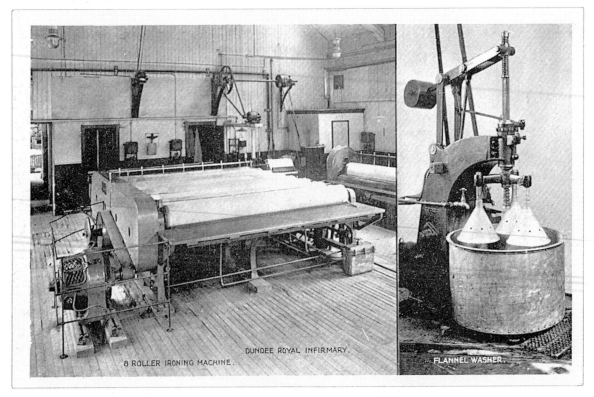

DUNDEE ROYAL INFIRMARY.

8 ROLLER IRONING MACHINE.

FLANNEL WASHER.

The latest in laundry technology at the DRI pictured in 1925. Acute services at the Royal were gradually shifted to the new hospital at Ninewells, which was completed between 1968 and 1974. The Royal closed completely in the 1990s, an example of health services shifting from central locations to peripheral sites with poor public transport links, in defiance of the fact that the chronically sick and infirm are often the poorest in society.

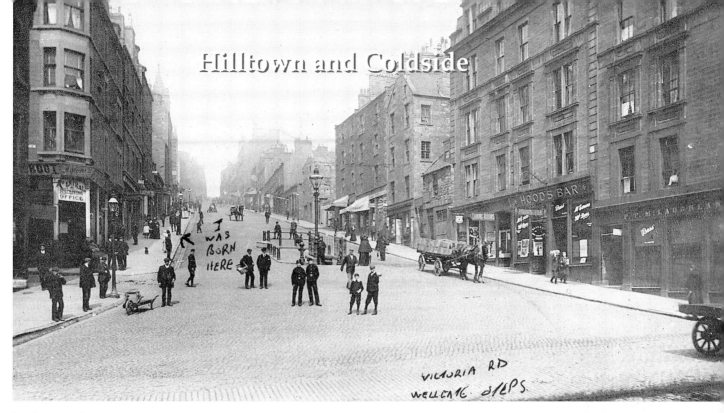

Looking up the precipitous Hilltown from Victoria Road in the early years of the last century. The Lady Well, from which the Wellgate derives its name, was located in this area. This was one of the city's principal wells, and analysis of the water in 1868 revealed it to be 'nothing but thoroughly purified sewage'. It lay close to an abattoir. The hill was so steep that a pool of horses was kept at the foot to provide extra muscle power when needed by carters.

The Hilltown was served by the single deck trams of the Constitution Road route, one of which is shown in this 1908 view. The savings bank building at the corner of Stirling Street on the left is still standing, as is the four storey tenement beyond it. This is dated 1905, although the soft nature of Dundee's sandstone (one writer described it as 'puddingy') often makes its tenements appear of greater antiquity than they really are. The tall chimney belonged to Stevenson Brothers' Dundee Dye Works, which relocated to their Hilltown site in 1881 from premises in Forebank Road.

The top of the Hilltown was the only part to escape the developers and this 1930s view is still recognisable, although the building on the corner of Kinghorne Road, left foreground, has been demolished. A gift from Baillie Charles Barrie, the Hilltown clock was erected in 1900. Its movement was made by G. D. Rattray of Nethergate and the case and plinth were cast at Beath & Keay's Dundee foundry. The Barony of Hilltown was purchased by Dundee and annexed in 1697. Its original name was Bonnet Hill as many of its inhabitants were engaged in bonnet-making. By the late eighteenth century the majority of the city's handloom linen weavers were concentrated in the Hilltown.

Robert Beat took over the fish merchant's shop of James Keiller at 90 Ann Street, Hilltown, in 1904. By 1926 the business was being run by his widow and in the early 1930s it moved across the street to No. 105. Around 1950 it was sold to Mrs I. Mitchell.

Most of the tenements in this 1910 view of Alexander Street from the corner of North Wellington Street were erected in the 1880s. Those in the left foreground have gone, and the other side of the street has also been cleared and is now dominated by the massive Maxwelltown, Carnegie and Jamaica towers, erected in 1968.

Another view of Alexander Street in the 1920s. Only the block of tenements with arched windows at the corner of North Ellen Street is still standing.

In 1833 Harry Walker was one of the very first manufacturers to employ whale oil for the softening of jute fibres. The following year he opened the first part of the Caldrum Works in St Salvador Street. The Franco–Prussian war of 1870–71 led to a boom in the jute trade and in 1872 Harry Walker & Sons had a vast new Caldrum Works erected. The complex was designed by the Dundee engineering firm of Robertson & Orchar of Wallace Foundry. It was the first textile mill in Britain to integrate spinning, weaving and finishing in one single unit, and the huge single-storey building contained six mills and six factories. The upper illustration shows dinner hour at the Caldrum Works in 1908, the lower one depicts the same gateway a couple of years later when it had been topped with office buildings.

The jute manufacturer A. D. Grimmond came to Dundee from Blairgowrie and opened the Bowbridge Works in Dens Road in 1857. They were enlarged in 1885, again by Robertson & Orchar. In 1972 the mill was still producing textiles, at which time it was one of five former jute factories owned by Jute Industries Ltd., although the building had been demolished by 1984. The magnificent sculpture of the company emblem of a camel, seen surmounting the gateway in this 1910 view, now reposes in the United States.

Nothing remains of the left-hand side of Strathmartine Road as seen in this view taken around 1912. The location is a short way up the street from the Hilltown clock. The white cottage with its gable projecting onto the pavement is typical of the weavers' rows which were concentrated in this area towards the end of the eighteenth century, and which were built end-on to the road.

STRATHMARTIN RD.

An advertising postcard for A. Kerr's Fairfield Dairy, which was located at 216 Strathmartine Road. The business was established in 1899 but lasted only fifteen years. This postcard was probably produced for promotional purposes, although it is unlikely that a picture of a muddy yard would encourage today's hygiene-conscious public to buy dairy products!

The tenements in Hill Street off Strathmartine Road survived the zeal of the redevelopers, but they were better built than most. Unusually for Dundee they were made of hammer-dressed ashlar – i.e. sandstone cut into regular rectangular blocks and chipped to create texture. Seen here in 1908, this was one of the better districts of the Hilltown as its high elevation (a glimpse of the Law is afforded at the top) meant it was less prone to pollution from the proliferation of factory chimneys in the area.

Paterson Street takes its name from the proprietor of the Law Mill, the chimneys of which dominate this 1907 view. The mill was built in 1838 and was one of the first jute and spinning mills in the city to employ power looms. These were first used in Dundee in 1836. Around the same period, the Law Mill became the first such establishment in Dundee to set up its own dyeworks for jute carpets. Later named the Lawside Works, the factory was considerably enlarged in both the 1860s and 1880s.

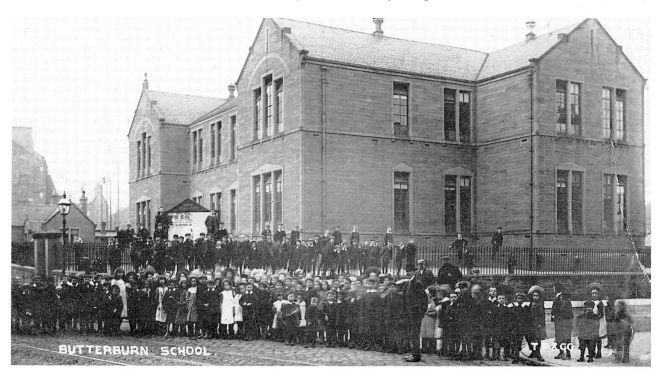

Another 1907 view, this time depicting Butterburn School which stood at 96 Strathmartine Road. Canning Street leads off to the right. The school opened in 1875 and was designed by David Maclaren. It was one of a number of schools erected in Dundee around this date to cope with the additional need for accommodation created by the passing of the 1872 Education Act (Scotland). This Act made it compulsory for every child to attend school between the ages of five and thirteen. The school closed in 1961 as tenement clearances depopulated the area. Butterburn Square now occupies the site.

The development of Coldside began at the end of the nineteenth century. Giving names to individual closes of tenements was a peculiarity of Dundee builders; in Glasgow and Edinburgh it was only entire blocks which were given additional names to those of the streets in which they were situated. The corner block in this 1910 picture is dated 1903 and the closes next door are named and dated as follows: Cluny Place (1895), Atholl Bank (1896), Hill View (1896), and St Ann's Place.

Coldside library was designed in 1908 by Frank Thomson, and the similarity between the main entrances to this and his earlier building at Blackness (seen on page 66) are obvious. Motorists, however, have no time to pause and admire his sophisticated curvilinear building as they whizz round the ring road roundabout which now occupies the foreground of this picture, taken shortly after the library's completion. The Law Mill in Paterson Street can be glimpsed to the rear. From 1939 to 1973 the Odeon cinema stood at 146 Strathmartine Road in the area to the left of and behind the library. Its site is now taken by a Lidl supermarket.

Thomson's pub on the left, now C. Barton's, and the tenements on the right are all that survive from this 1920s view of Dundonald Street. The Dura Street jute mills are visible in the background. There were several jute works concentrated in Dura Street, the first of which was founded in 1836 by Scott & Sons (it was demolished in 1985). Next came Malcolm Ogilvie's Constable Works for the weaving of linen and jute, which dated from 1846. These were extended in 1851 and supplemented by a finishing works in Arthurstone Terrace in 1888. Laing & Buist opened the Stobswell Works in Dura Street in 1862. They were demolished in 1985.

This imposing Sentinel steam lorry belonged to Robertson & Orchar in the 1920s. The company owned the Wallace Foundry in Maitland Street and designed and built many of the city's largest jute factories. They also made many components for the shipbuilding industry. In the 1930s they merged with the rival firm of Urquhart & Lindsay, who owned the Blackness Foundry. The combined firm was known by the acronym ULRO, but closed in the 1960s.

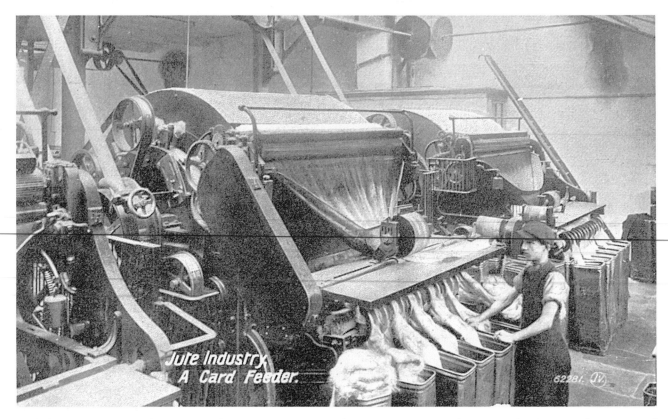

Both these pictures were taken in a Dundee jute mill in 1909. The first stage of jute manufacture involved passing the compacted bales through a jute opener, which softened the fibre to a certain extent and got it into a suitable condition to pass through the jute softener. This contained around sixty fluted rollers, and as the jute passed between them pipes sprinkled it with oil and water. It was then fed through the breaker cards, machines with large cylinders comprising wooden staves covered with steel teeth, around which smaller cylinders, also covered with teeth, were positioned. This process discharged a continuous fibre called 'sliver'. The sliver was then passed through machines called finisher cards, making the fibre finer still, after which roving frames twisted it. Next it was spun into thread on spinning frames, then wound onto bobbins known as cops by cop winding machines. These were taken to the weaving department where the thread was woven into cloth on power looms.

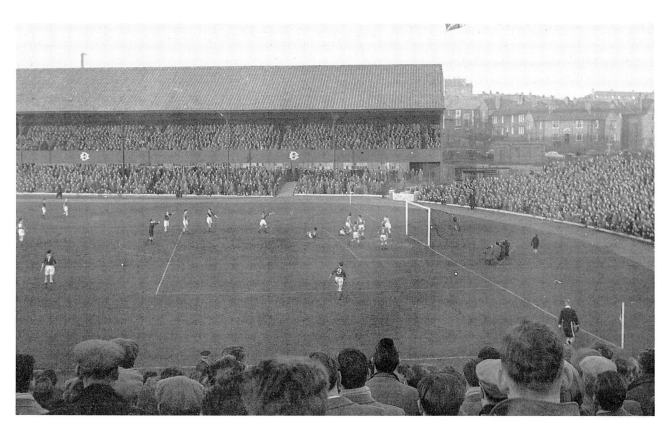

What appears to be a capacity crowd watches Dundee FC in this 1957 view of Dens Park. Dundee was formed by the merger of two teams, Our Boys and East End, both founded in 1877, and was admitted to the Scottish League in 1893. Our Boys played at West Craigie Park in the west end; East End's ground was Clepington Park, now Tannadice. For a time Dundee played at West Craigie before moving to Carolina Port near the docks. Financial ills led to the reorganisation of the club and in 1898 it leased a plot of farmland at Dens Road. It purchased this in 1919 on hearing a rumour that a neighbouring engineering works was bidding for the site. In the same year the ground was remodelled by Archie Leitch, a famous name in stadium design.

This 'group of Arabs', as they are styled on this 1905 postcard, illustrates the degree of poverty evident in the city at the time. 'Arabs' is the nickname of fans of Dundee's other football team, United. Originating from a team called Dundee Harp, renamed Dundee Hibernian in 1894, their name changed to Dundee United in 1923. When admitted to the league in 1909 the club had need of a permanent ground and attention turned to Clepington Park, then home to Dundee Wanderers. Although successful in ousting Wanderers, the displaced team responded by removing everything from the ground, including the goalposts. Hibernian inherited an empty field. Tannadice Park opened in 1909.

A Group of Arabs

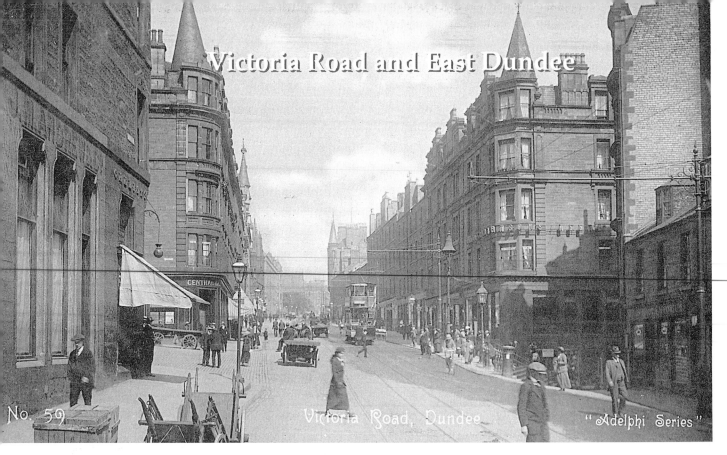

No. 59   Victoria Road, Dundee   "Adelphi Series"

Victoria Road was created in 1884 by the major widening of what had been Bucklemaker Wynd, a steep vennel of slums. Craftsmen tended to group together and the buckle-makers were members of the Hammermen, one of the Nine Trades. The Wellgate Steps are on the right, and the foot of Hilltown on the left of this 1914 view. The Wellgate library now occupies the site of the turreted tenement on the right. Opened in 1978, it superseded the public library in the Albert Institute. The Central Bar on the left was known briefly as the Top o' the Stairs before demolition in the 1970s. Next door, A. & S. Henry's ornate calendar (finishing) works is still standing. Built in 1874–75, it was restored in 1997.

The Victoria United Presbyterian Church, on the left of this 1910 view of Victoria Street, was erected in 1874. It became the headquarters of the Boys' Brigade in the 1960s. By the 1860s the extent of Baxter's Linen Works had become such that tunnels were constructed under Victoria Street, Dens Road and Princes Street to link the different mills.

The construction of the north-east radial route has devastated Princes Street, seen here in 1920. The savings bank on the right was built in 1914 and was converted into Trinity Church Hall in 1985. Princes Street was laid out by 1821 and building soon began at the bottom end, around David Baxter's Lower Dens Works (1822). By 1834 it was either developed or feued along its entire length. A concentration of mills in the area meant it was once the busiest street outside the centre of Dundee, with over a hundred shops.

Looking up Princes Street c.1912. On 20 January 1889 William Henry Bury and his wife arrived in Dundee from London and obtained keys to view a property at 113 Princes Street. Mr Bury did not return them and it transpired he had basically squatted there for three weeks. It later emerged that a neighbour had heard screams coming from the flat on 4 February. A week later Bury handed himself over to the police, who later reported at his trial he had uttered the words 'I'm Jack the Ripper'. His wife had been strangled and had vicious stab wounds to her abdomen. Bury slept in the same room as her mutilated body for seven nights. He was hanged in Dundee on 24 April 1889. The Ripper is thought to have committed between five and eight murders in London in 1888. There were no further killings after Bury's execution.

Baxter's had attempted to open a school in the Lower Dens Works in 1828, but it had met with little interest, although a later attempt in 1841 attracted between 200 and 300 pupils from among their workforce. In 1858 they opened their half-time school in Crescent Street. This followed the passing of the 1844 Act introducing the half-time system of education for child workers from the ages of eight to fourteen. Mary Slessor was educated here during her time in Baxter's. The old school (illustrated here) was closed in 1905 and became incorporated in Wallacetown School.

A white-gloved policeman has no traffic to direct in this 1920 view of Albert Street, looking from Arbroath Road. The tenements in the foreground were built in the 1880s; the ones in the middle distance on the left with bay windows were constructed in 1900. A culvert carries a stream under the west side of Albert Street; this continues to the sea under the line of Peep o' Day Lane. Businesses have a struggle to survive in this part of the city, cut off from the centre by the virtually uncrossable East Marketgait.

The tenements have gone, but Wallacetown Parish Church looks the same as it did when this postcard was produced in 1905. Built in 1843 to serve the spiritual needs of the growing industrial population of the area, it is now known as Trinity Church.

A still familiar view of Stobswell dating from the 1920s and showing Albert Street on the left and the junction of Dura Street on the right. Ogilvie Church was erected in 1898–99 and designed by Leslie Ower. It was renamed Stobswell Church c.1990 on the amalgamation of three local churches.

Looking down Albert Street, with Pitkerro Road leading off to the left. The imposing curved tenement is inscribed Simpson Place. This 1920s view comes from the Wilmar series of postcards, a contraction of the name of the publisher, William MacLean Ross. Three generations of the family traded under the same name and ran wholesale and retail stationery businesses in a succession of premises from *c*.1910 until 1983. The postcards were published from before the First World War until *c*.1950 and depicted suburban Dundee streets often overlooked by the larger publishers.

Forfar Road has changed little since this 1909 view was taken, except that it is now busier and the right-hand side is dominated by the burned shell of Morgan Academy. The first horse trams ran to Morgan Hospital (Academy) in 1880, with another line branching along Arbroath Road to Baxter Park. The city's first electric trams ran along Forfar Road to the Maryfield terminus on 6 March 1901, the service ceasing in 1956.

Morgan Academy, on the left of this 1909 postcard, was opened in 1868 under the name Morgan Hospital. It was founded with a bequest from John Morgan dating from 1850, and was intended as a boarding school for the sons of 180 artisans and tradesmen. Morgan's will was contested and the case was taken to the Court of Session by the Nine Trades. The trustees were victorious in upholding the will, but the cost of the legal battle depleted the fund, after which it was only sufficient to support 60 scholars. Construction of the academy began in 1863.

So-called Morgan Hospital was designed in a French chateau baronial style by the architects Peddie & Kinnear. Control of the school passed to Dundee School Board in 1887, when it was renamed Morgan Academy. At that time it ceased to be a boarding school and was redesigned internally to provide classroom accommodation for 650 pupils. In March 2001 fire tore through the A-listed building. By the time it was brought under control the school had been almost completely gutted, with only part of one wing of the quadrangular structure saved. Fortunately, Dundee has finally woken to the benefits of conservation and the building is currently undergoing restoration.

This view of the corner of Baldovan Terrace and Park Avenue dates from 1920. The tenements in Park Avenue, Morgan Place and Baxter Park Terrace were built in 1901 on what had been West Craigie Park. This had been laid out as a football ground and was home to Our Boys, forerunners of Dundee FC and in existence from 1882–93. It was the club's first pitch, but was used for only a few months before it was given up in favour of Carolina Port, after which it was taken over by Dundee Harp, precursors to Dundee United.

A crowd of 70,000 gathered to watch the official opening of Baxter Park by the Prime Minister, Earl Russell, in September 1863. It was a gift to the people from jute magnate David Baxter, knighted in 1864. The plans were drawn up in 1859 by Sir Joseph Paxton, the designer of the Crystal Palace and much in demand for laying out formal city parks and country estates. The pavilion in this Edwardian view was the work of G. H. Stokes, Paxton's son-in-law.

Pleasure Boats on Stobsmuir Pond, Dundee.

Dundee's first piped public water supply was drawn from Stobsmuir and Monikie in the 1840s under the auspices of the 1845 Dundee Water Act. The 'Stobie' later became a popular recreation ground. During the Second World War the pond was filled in so it would not reflect moonlight and alert enemy aircraft to the blacked-out city. It was re-excavated after the war. Small dinghies and paddle boats were a popular feature at Stobsmuir from the 1920s through to the 1960s, when a sail on the pond cost fourpence. During the winter, when the pond froze over, it was a favourite place for skating.

Miss Joan Phillips ran the Newbigging Dairy in the 1920s. It was situated at 36 Watson Street, between the Arbroath and Broughty Ferry Roads.

Sylvan beauty in an Edwardian view of Arbroath Road, looking east from Dalgleish Road. When this postcard was produced *c.*1910 this was on the very edge of the city. Beyond the trees on the left lies the Eastern Necropolis, opened in 1863 as a replacement for the 'Howff' in the city centre. The houses of Craigiebank now occupy the right-hand side of a much wider Arbroath Road. The housing scheme was designed in 1919 by James Thomson and his son Harry.

Musing on my many years of collecting old picture postcards, I cannot actually recall having read the message 'wish you were here' on any of the many thousands I have handled. This is just as well in this case, as the card features a view of the city slaughterhouses in Ferry Road. The buildings date from the 1870s when the City Improvement Act removed abattoirs from the city centre. Many were congregated around the end of the Murraygate, and panicked animals making a last bid for freedom were a commonplace hazard for residents in the area.

A view of Baxter's jute mills taken from the Dundee gasworks in the early 1950s. William Baxter arrived from Glamis in 1822 and erected the Lower Dens Mill in Princes Street for the weaving of linen. In 1830 he opened the St Roque's Mill, and introduced power looms six years later. The vast Upper Dens Mill, with its Italianate bellcote, was erected in 1865–66. By 1890 Baxter's was the world's largest linen manufacturer and at its peak had a workforce of 5,000. Taken over by Low & Bonar Ltd. in 1924, further expansion followed with completion of the North Mill in 1935. Business declined in the 1960s due to overseas competition and the works closed in 1974. In the 1990s the Upper Dens Mill was converted into flats, many of which enjoy enviable views of the city.

Broughty Ferry Road seen from the corner of South Baffin Street around 1910. This block of tenements was erected in 1891, and the sub-post office at the far end was opened on 1 May the same year. The row is unusual in that the buildings are steel framed, the girders being supplied by the Caledon Shipyard, whose workers the flats were intended to house.

Lochee

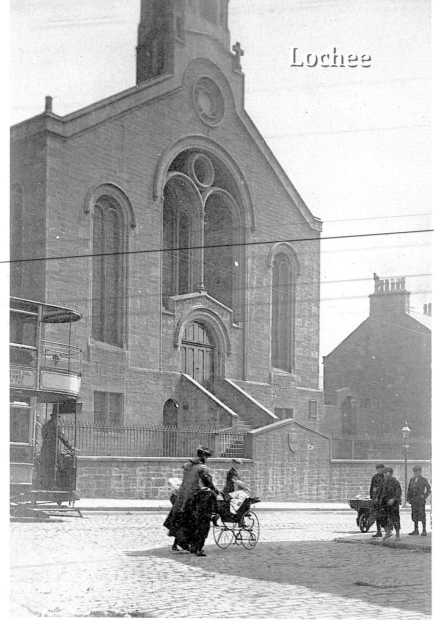

A sunlit study of Dudhope Church at 113 Lochee Road in the early years of last century. Erected in 1840, the church closed in 1953. After the Foresters Halls in Nicoll Street burned down in 1963 (following refurbishment only six months earlier), the Dundee Repertory Theatre moved into Dudhope Church, remaining there until 1981. The 'Rep', which launched the careers of many who are now household names through their work in cinema and television, moved into its much-deserved custom-built home in Tay Square in 1982. The old church has since been pulled down.

Lochee is traditionally believed to have been founded as a village of handloom linen weavers in the employ of a bleacher named Cock, who is said to have arrived in the area *c.*1700. Other sources give the date of foundation as the 1730s, which may be more likely as linen weaving was becoming a more important industry in Scotland by this period. Whatever the precise date, by 1777 David Cock, a descendent, was employing some 280 looms. In 1859 Dundee expanded its boundaries to encompass Lochee, which by that date was a substantial town. The buildings to the rear of Cobden Street, visible on the hill in the background, are the only structures remaining from this 1910 view. When the Stone of Destiny was stolen from Westminster Abbey in the 1950s, it is said to have reposed for a time in St Columba's Church, on the left.

Logie Street, Lochee

This 1907 view depicts Lochee library and public baths, opened in 1896. Both the baths and library were paid for by Thomas Hunter Cox of Duncarse. The splendid Jacobean building by J. Murray & Robertson has recently been refurbished.

The building in the foreground on the right and the corner tenement on the left of this 1905 view of High Street were demolished to make way for the Lochee bypass. In 1885 a steam tramway was inaugurated from Dundee High Street to Lochee. Dundee Corporation took over the running of the city tramways in 1899 and electrification was introduced on the Lochee route in 1900.

The Dundee Savings Bank building on the right was designed by David Baxter in 1903 and is one of a number of banks built to his plans around the city. Everything on the other side of the street in this Edwardian view has now gone, bulldozed to make way for the Highgate shopping centre in the 1960s. It is as ugly a mall as is to be found anywhere, and the redevelopers failed to capitalise on an opportunity to widen and pedestrianise the narrow street. Both the City Churches and old Town House were demolished to relieve unemployment. The jobless total is high in Lochee and the same solution might well be applied to the Highgate.

Parish Church, Lochee

By 1829 the population of Lochee had grown sufficiently to merit the building of a parish church, and St Ninians was designed by the architect David Neave. This simple but elegant Georgian church still looks as it did when this 1905 picture was taken.

In 1793 the Cock family name was changed to Cox. Seventeen years later, in 1810, the family firm underwent major expansion and became a pioneer in the manufacture of jute cloth, becoming Cox Brothers in 1841. Ten years later the first part of their vast Camperdown Works was completed. This was the High Mill, on the left of this Edwardian photograph. There followed a calendaring (finishing) mill, completed in 1865 and reputed to contain the largest calendaring machine in Europe. The famous polychrome chimney known as Cox's Stack, on the right of the picture, was designed by James Maclaren and George Cox. An urban myth grew in Dundee that the top of the stack was so wide a horse and cart could be driven round it, but this was quite apocryphal. Cox's eventually covered a 35 acre site and was the largest jute mill in the world. Following closure of the works in 1981 much of the site was redeveloped with housing and entertainment facilities. The stack, long threatened with demolition, was reprieved and remains a prominent landmark on the Lochee skyline.

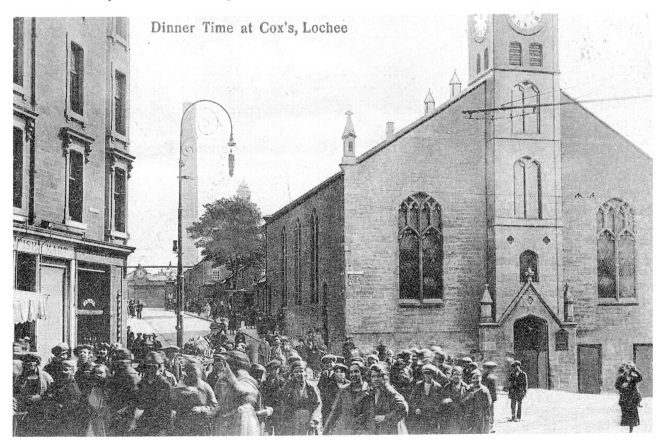

Dinner Time at Cox's, Lochee

West High Street is one of the few parts of the old town centre to have survived the developers relatively unscathed, although the East Church in the centre of this 1906 view was demolished in 1960 and a branch of Woolworths now stands on the site. The Albert Bar in the right foreground is the oldest hostelry in Lochee, founded in 1850 as the Albert Hotel and Brewery.

Between 1841 and 1851 the population of Lochee quadrupled owing to an abundance of work in the expanding Camperdown Works. Many of the new workers were Irish immigrants who came to Scotland in the wake of the potato famine of 1845–46, which is estimated to have claimed over a million lives. Many of the immigrants and their descendants were housed in this redbrick row which earned the nickname Tipperary. The majority of the Irish were Roman Catholics and their influx led to the establishment of St Mary's Church, Lochee, in 1865.

South Road, seen here in 1910, has been almost entirely demolished. Huge multi-storey blocks built from 1960–62 now occupy the right-hand side of the street.

Central Lochee retained much of the character of a Forfarshire mill town into the 1950s. Bank Street linked the High Street to South Road, and is shown here around 1930. The buildings of Bank Street have been erased under a roundabout and wide straight road, and even the street name has now gone.

The car terminus at Lochee, photographed in 1907. The Lochee, Perth Road and Maryfield routes were the final sections of Dundee's tramway network to be closed on 21 October 1956. Thousands lined the streets to witness the passage of the city's last trams. The wall on the right of the picture surrounded Harefield House, the mansion of jute magnate James Cox, which was designed in 1844 by James Maclaren. Although its grounds have been much encroached upon, the house is the last of Dundee's 'jute palaces', the others having succumbed to developers or dry rot. Liff Road School behind the High Street tram was built in the 1870s, but demolished prior to 1974 to make way for a police station.

Ancrum Road School is a 1905 enlargement and remodelling of an earlier school. The new building was designed by J. H. Langlands and the Dundee School Board architect W. G. Lamond. This was the first of many of Lamond's subdued art nouveau designs, and the stepped tiers of stairwell windows on the left are suggestive of Mackintosh. It is a comparatively scarce style in Scotland and Lamond's schools form an interesting group.

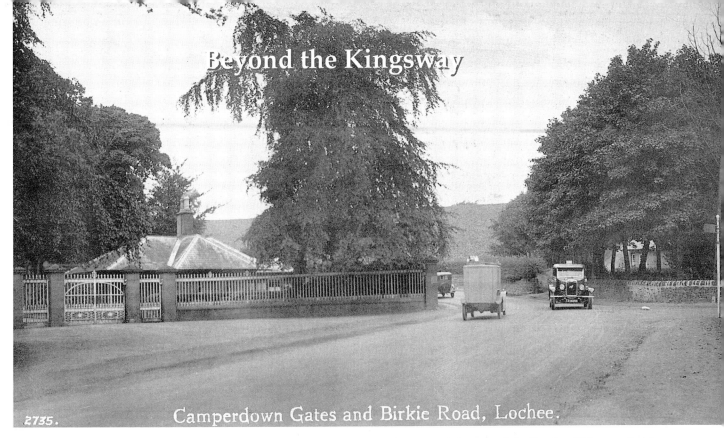

2735. Camperdown Gates and Birkie Road, Lochee.

On 11 October 1797 ships under the command of Admiral Adam Duncan (1731–1804) engaged the Dutch off Kamperdoen. After a bloody but decisive battle Duncan captured seven ships, including two flagships. This victory earned him the title of Viscount Duncan of Camperdown, the Dutch name being anglicised. A mansion house by the same name was designed for his descendants in 1824 by the eminent architect William Burn. The Camperdown estate was purchased by Dundee Corporation using money bequeathed by Sir James K. Caird, and formally opened as a public park by Princess Elizabeth in 1946. This view of the lodge dates from 1930.

A picture of berry-picking at Downfield fruit farm, featured on a 1922 postcard advertising Thyne & Sons shop at 8–10 Union Street, Dundee. At this time Downfield and neighbouring Baldovan were small villages some three miles from the city, dependant on fruit-farming and agriculture. Since the last war the rural character has been swamped by council estates and suburban bungalow-land.

STRATHMARTINE ROAD, DOWNFIELD   207

Downfield began to expand slowly during the second half of the nineteenth century as the middle classes departed the city and its smoke, although it was Broughty Ferry which saw the greatest expansion in this period. These well-built homes in Strathmartine Road date from the 1870s to 1890s. By 1875 Downfield had grown sufficiently to merit the opening of a sub-post office. The village was annexed to Dundee in 1907, when the city boundary was enlarged to allow for future expansion. This deserted view dates from 1930.

A city centre bound tramcar, photographed at the Monifieth terminus of the Dundee, Broughty Ferry & District Tramway Company. The tram is a Dundee Corporation vehicle (the Corporation operated the route jointly with the Tramway Co.), and the photograph can be dated to *c.*1918 as conductresses were not employed with Dundee Corporation until 1917. The opening of the electric car route to Downfield in 1900 gave Dundonians the opportunity to get well away from the heart of the city for just 1*d.* It also gave workers and their children access to labouring, and, in season, berry picking and tattie howking, much-needed employment during the city's many recessions in the shipbuilding and jute industries. The Downfield tram route closed on 26 November 1955.

The construction of Mains Castle began around 1480. In the sixteenth century it became the seat of the Grahams of Fintry, and it was the fifth laird, Sir David Graham, who added the 70-foot library and stair tower in 1562. The fireplaces were added by the seventh laird in the 1730s, although Mains was abandoned as a residence in 1740. In recent years the ruins in this 1907 photograph received unwanted attention from vandals. However, the castle was completely restored to its original condition by Dundee District Council architects in the 1990s.

At the beginning of the eighteenth century Scotland's roads were unmaintained, frequently impassable, and a hindrance to communication and commerce. To alleviate the problem the government devised the turnpike system, whereby private companies would be set up to improve the roads and run them at a profit by levying tolls. Mains Toll, seen here in the 1920s, dates from the upgrading of the Dundee to Forfar Road to a turnpike in the 1760s. Although the system served its purpose, and much of Scotland's road network today owes its existence to the turnpikes, public dissatisfaction with the tolls grew. In 1878 an Act was passed abolishing road tolls and instructing each county to appoint its own surveyors and road boards.

Long vanished under the Ardler housing estate, this tiny bothy at Mains of Baldovan farm was home to all six of these lads *c*.1914. The bothy system for unmarried ploughmen and farm labourers spread rapidly into Tayside and Fife from the Lothians in the late eighteenth century. Even as late as this picture, the staple diet of bothy lads consisted of oatmeal, potatoes and milk. The one holding the bowl is probably preparing himself a bowl of brose from the communal pot. This was a dollop of oatmeal, boiling water, salt to taste, and milk. Few of these bothy shots are located, but invariably contain beer, jaw warmer pipes and a squeeze box.

The Caird Park was yet another of Sir James K. Caird's benefactions, and was formally opened by his sister Mrs Emma Grace Marryat in 1920. On 3 November 1923 she also opened the new public golf course. The clubhouse in this contemporary view is an early example of 'steading conversion', so popular in the 1990s. The former farmhouse with its pointed central gable is typical of Angus farmhouses of the 1850s.

It would not be fitting to conclude this book of old photographs and postcards without paying tribute to the firm of Valentine's of Dundee, which originally published more than a quarter of them. The history of the firm began in 1825 when John Valentine (1792–1868) gave up business as a linen manufacturer and turned his attentions to engraving printing blocks for the linen industry. His son James Valentine was made a partner in 1830. James was a portrait painter, and began producing political engravings which the firm printed as pictorial envelopes. Subjects included a campaign for the Universal Penny Post, and a notable series commissioned in 1849 by Elihu Burritt, an American philanthropist and anti-war campaigner. These are very rare and valuable items today. In the 1850s James travelled to France where he studied photography, and in 1856 he is noted as a studio photographer in Dundee.

Queen Victoria's love affair with Scotland began in the 1840s and culminated in the building of Balmoral Castle in 1853. The era of the Highland 'grand tour' had begun, and with it the demand for souvenirs. In 1863 James's eldest son William joined the company. An accomplished landscape photographer, it was probably he and his father James who took the first 1,700 photographs which were published in full and half plate, probably in 1878, the year the company's registers begin. By the time Valentine's became a limited company in 1896, this catalogue numbered nearly 26,000 views of the United Kingdom. Picture postcards, which had already been extremely popular in Europe for several years, were bound up in post office regulations in Britain. In 1894 these were relaxed, at which point Britain's first privately printed picture postcards were authorised. Still restricted in size and with the message only allowed on the picture side, they did not take the country by storm.

When Valentine began printing postcards is disputed. Some sources claim 1895, but a major survey of collectors has failed to turn up an example used before 1898. The size regulations were relaxed in 1899, and in 1902 the post office permitted the back of a postcard to be divided so the picture could cover the whole of the front. What followed by 1905 was a national passion for sending and collecting postcards. Valentine, in on the ground floor, had invested in each improvement in printing technology, and by 1906 was a market leader and floated as a public company, Valentine & Sons Ltd.

By 1910 (and quite possibly earlier) Valentine was the world's largest publisher of view postcards, with offices in Dublin, Cape Town, Melbourne and Montreal. Although views were the company's staple, many top artists also designed for Valentine, most notably Mabel Lucie Attwell, whose cutesy children ran to hundreds of designs. Ironically, she was a spinster who couldn't suffer kids. Even after the First World War when demand for postcards declined, Valentine retained the premier spot, competing for much of the Scottish trade with Dundee-based rival J. B. White. Valentine's moved from their Perth Road factory to new premises south of Kingsway in the 1950s (although they retained the Perth Road factory after the move). Postcard production continued with a series of most towns and villages in Britain until the 1960s. When monochrome postcards gave way to coloured glossies in 1967, the cost of printing meant only large runs were viable, and Valentine abandoned postcard production in 1970. Continuing as stationery and greetings card manufacturers, the firm subsequently closed their Dundee factory and transferred operations to their Dublin factory.

FURTHER READING

The books listed below were used by the authors during their research. None of them are available from Stenlake Publishing. Those interested in finding out more are advised to contact their local bookshop or reference library.

anon., *Dundee, Fifty Years of Progress 1900–1950*
Alexander, John, *Dundee Pubs, Past and Present*, 1992
Cronshaw, Andrew, *Old Dundee Picture Postcards*, 1988
Dundee Corporation, *Dundee and Round About*, 1964
Kay, Billy (ed.), *The Dundee Book*, 1990
Marshall, Peter, *The Railways of Dundee*, 1996
McCraw, Ian, *The Fairs of Dundee*, 1994
MacMurchie, David A., *I Remember Another Princes Street*, 1986
McKean C. & Walker D., *Dundee, An Illustrated Architectural Guide*, 1993

Sinclair, David, *A History of the Tay Ferries 1713–1966*, 1996
Smith, W. J. (ed.), *A History of Dundee*, 1873
Smout, T. C., *A History of the Scottish People*, 1969
Smout, T. C., *A Century of the Scottish People*, 1987
Somner, David, *A History of the DP&L and Associated Companies*, 1995
Watson, Norman, *Dundee in Old Picture Postcards*, 1997
Whatley C. A., Swinfen D. B., Smith A. M., *The Life and Times of Dundee*, 1993